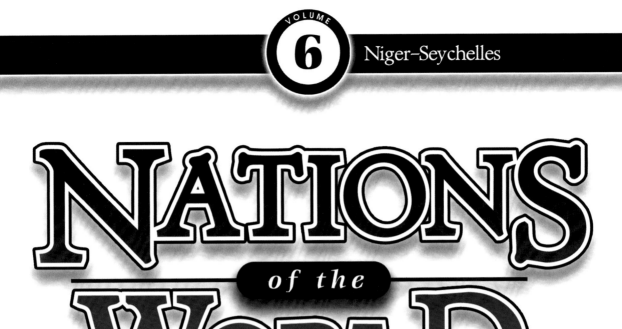

NATIONS of the WORLD

SAMUEL BRIMSON

Library of Congress Cataloging-in-Publication Data available
upon request from publisher. Fax (414) 336-0157 for the attention
of the Publishing Records Department.

ISBN 0-8368-5490-X

This North American edition first published in 2004 by
World Almanac® Library,
330 West Olive Street, Suite 100, Milwaukee, WI 53212 USA.

Created by Trocadero Publishing, an Electra Media Group
Enterprise, Suite 204, 74 Pitt Street, Sydney NSW 2000, Australia.

Original copyright © 2003 S. and L. Brodie.

WORLD ALMANAC® LIBRARY

Niger

REPUBLIC OF NIGER

The Republic of Niger is located in western Africa. The northern sixty percent of the country is the harsh Sahara Desert. The central region is semiarid and lightly wooded. Much of the south is a fertile, forested area. The Niger River Valley of the southwest is the best for farming and human habitation. The south has a wet season from June to October, whereas the north sees little rainfall.

The dominant ethnic group is the Hausa. They make up sixty percent of the population. The Hausa, along with the Djerma, are farmers in the south. The Fulani and Tuareg are nomads. Nearly all of the people are Muslims. French is the official language. Hausa and other indigenous languages are in widespread use.

Human occupation of Niger dates back to about 1000 B.C. It was on the path of a major caravan route from North Africa to the southern empires of Mali and Songhai. The Hausa states were dominant in southern Niger until the Fulani seized them in the nineteenth century. Tuareg nomads built a capital at Agadez, while the Songhai Empire ruled in western areas.

French explorers in the late eighteenth century were followed by Germans in 1850. The 1884–85 Conference of Berlin allocated Niger to France. Military outposts established in the 1890s met fierce Tuareg resistance. Niger was made a military territory in 1900. It became a French overseas territory in 1946. Little economic or social development occurred.

Niger remained within the French Community until 1958. It became independent on August 3, 1960. Hamani Diori was elected president. Stability prevailed despite the poor economy and the devastating 1968–1973 Saharan drought. Lt. Col. Seyni Kountché deposed Diori in April of 1974.

Demand for uranium in the early 1980s brought prosperity to some citizens of Niger. A severe drop in uranium prices in the late eighties once again weakened the economy.

Civilian Mahamane Ousman was elected president in 1993. A peace agreement brought an end to a five-year-long rebellion by the Tuaregs. They were given increased autonomy within the country.

Colonel Ibrahim Baré Mainarrara led a coup against Ousman in January of 1996. He arrested opponents, filled the electorate with his friends and got himself elected president. He was assassinated by members of his presidential guard in April 1999.

Tandja Mamadou was elected president in November of 1999. Foreign aid resumed becauseNiger had returned to civilian rule.

GOVERNMENT
Website www.nigerembassyusa.org
Capital Niamey
Type of government Republic
Independence from France
August 3, 1960
Voting Universal adult suffrage
Head of state President
Head of government President
Constitution 1993
Legislature
Unicameral National Assembly
Judiciary State Court
Member of IMF, OAU, UN,
UNESCO, WHO, WTO

LAND AND PEOPLE
Land area
489,190 sq mi (1,267,000 sq km)
Highest point Mt. Bagzane
6,234 ft (1,900 m)
Population 10,355,176
Major cities and populations
Niamey 731,000
Zinder 120,000
Ethnic groups
Hausa 56%, Djerma 22%, Fulani
8%, Tuareg 8%
Religions
Islam 95%
Languages
French (official), indigenous
languages

ECONOMIC
Currency CFA franc
Industry
mining, cement, textiles, food
processing, chemicals
Agriculture
cotton, peanuts, millet, sorghum,
tapioca, rice, cattle, sheep, goats,
horses, poultry
Natural resources
uranium, coal, iron ore, tin,
phosphates, gold, petroleum

Nigeria

FEDERAL REPUBLIC OF NIGERIA

GOVERNMENT
Website www.nopa.net
Capital Abuja
Type of government Republic
Independence from Britain
October 1, 1960
Voting Universal adult suffrage
Head of state and **government**
President
Constitution 1999
Legislature
Bicameral National Assembly
House of Representatives (lower house), Senate (upper house)
Judiciary Supreme Court
Member of CN, IMF, OAU, OPEC, UN, UNESCO, UNHCR, WHO, WTO

LAND AND PEOPLE
Land area 356,669 sq mi
(923,768 sq km)
Highest point
Mt. Dimlang 6,700 ft (2,042 m)
Coastline 532 mi (853 km)
Population 126,635,626
Major cities and populations
Lagos 1,700,000
Ibadan 1,600,000
Ogbomosho 800,000
Ethnic groups Hausa, Fulani, Yoruba, Ibo, Kanuri, Tiv, Edo, Nuep, Ibidio
Religions Islam 50%, Christianity 40%, traditional animism 10%
Languages
English (official), Hausa and other indigenous languages

ECONOMIC
Currency Naira
Industry
mining, palm oil, oil refining, nuts, cotton, rubber, wood, textiles, cement, food products, footwear, chemicals, fertilizer, ceramics, steel
Agriculture
cacao, nuts, palm oil, corn, rice, sorghum, millet, tapioca, yams, rubber, cattle, sheep, goats, pigs
Natural resources
natural gas, petroleum, tin, columbite, iron ore, coal, limestone, lead, zinc

Nigeria is on the Gulf of Guinea in western Africa. The coast is dominated by the swamps and lagoons of the Niger River delta. Beyond the coast is a belt of tropical forests. The central grassland plateau leads north to the Sahara Desert. The climate is tropical, with high temperatures and humidity year round. Rainfall is heaviest in the south.

Nigeria, Africa's most populous country, has more than 250 ethnic groups. The largest are the Hausa, Fulani, Yoruba and Ibo. Half of the population is Muslim. Forty percent is Christian. The rest follow traditional animist beliefs. Hausa, Yoruba and Ibo are the most common languages. English is the official language.

Evidence of Stone Age cultures has been uncovered in Nigeria. The Nok civilization in the Jos Plateau region became known for fine quality terracotta sculptures around 500 B.C. The state of Kanem-Bornu expanded south into Nigeria in the eleventh century A.D. Heavily fortified Hausa city-states were created at Kano, Zaria and Katsina during the same period. These city-states became important posts along the route through the Sahara. Merchants traded gold and cotton as well as slaves. Trade contact spread Islam throughout the land.

The Portuguese and British arrived during the seventeenth and eighteenth centuries. They established slave-trading settlements in the Niger River delta area. Palm oil dominated Lagos commerce after Britain banned slave trading in the 1830s. Britain annexed Lagos in 1861 to block attempts at slave trading by other countries.

Further British colonization was carried out by the Royal Niger Company, formed in 1886. Britain established a protectorate over the area. The kingdom of Benin in the southwest and further lands in the southeast were added. It became the Protectorate of South Nigeria in 1900.

The area was divided into the Eastern, Western and Northern regions. Eight years later they merged into a single colony. Railways were built and agriculture developed.

Nigerian demands for self-government after World War II resulted in a series of short-lived constitutions. A timetable for independence was agreed upon and a constitution established in 1954. A federal system was chosen, to give the many ethnic groupings some autonomy. Nigeria became independent on October 1, 1960 and was

Nigeria

admitted to the U.N. the same year. The first prime minister, Sir Abubakar Tafawa Balewa, represented the major parties of the northern and western regions. The governor-general was Nnamdi Azikiwe, who became president when Nigeria was declared a republic in 1963.

Major General Johnson Aguiyi-Ironsi assumed the presidency after a 1966 military coup caused by ethnic strife. A member of the Ibo people, he suspended federal and state constitutions and massacred political leaders. He was assassinated in a coup by Hausa military officers six months later. Many Ibo were killed or forced to flee. Lieutenant-Colonel Yakubu Gowon became president.

Lieutenant Colonel Chukwuemeka Ojukwu led the eastern region's fight for independence. It declared itself the Republic of Biafra in 1967. Three years of bitter fighting ensued. Images of starving Biafrans shocked the world. The rebels surrendered in January 1970.

Nigeria's economy was booming as a result of increasing oil exports. Unfortunately, the benefits flowed to a corrupt elite in government and business. Gowon was deposed in 1975 by General Murtala

Muhammad. He was in turn assassinated in 1976 and replaced by General Olusegun Obasanjo. The government introduced repressive laws to curb rebel movements.

Alhaji Shehu Shagari became president in civilian elections of 1979. He was deposed by the military in 1983. Major General Ibrahim Babangida introduced a new constitution in 1990. He annulled the 1992 presidential poll, after his opponent, Moshood Abiola, took the lead. Abiola was imprisoned after he called for an uprising to out the military government.

Another military coup brought Gen. Sani Abacha to power. Abacha banned labor unions and political parties. Widespread international condemnation followed the execution of nine human rights

activists. Among them was renowned author Ken Saro-Wira. Nigeria was expelled from the Commonwealth of Nations. Corporations were severely criticized for continuing to invest in Nigeria.

Abacha died in 1998. His replacement, General Abdulsalam Abubakar, freed many political prisoners. News of the death in prison of Moshood Abiola, winner of the 1992 election, sparked widespread rioting.

Local and national elections were held in 1998 and 1999. The new president was General Obasanjo, one of the freed prisoners. He had engineered the return of civilian rule in 1979. The Commonwealth of Nations restored Nigeria's membership in 1999.

The Durbar Festival is held at Kano each year.

Niue

One of the largest coral islands in the world, Niue is located in the southern Pacific Ocean. It has a central plateau with limestone cliffs inland from the coast. The climate is tropical with high temperatures and humidity throughout the year.

More Niuean people live outside the country than inside. The present population is about 2,000 people, having dropped from 5,000 in the 1960s. More than 18,000 Niuean people live in New Zealand. Christianity is the dominant religion. The Niuean language is closely related to Tongan and Samoan.

Polynesian peoples from Samoa and Tonga settled on the island around A.D. 900. Captain James Cook led the first Europeans to land here, during an exploration of the Pacific Ocean. He named it Savage Island because of the reception he received from its people.

The London Missionary Society established itself on Niue in 1846. Most of the population was converted to Christianity within the next ten years. Slave traders from Peru staged regular raids on the population in the 1860s. Europeans gradually established a cotton-growing industry.

Britain annexed Niue in 1900. Initially it was administered by New Zealand as part of the Cook Islands. A resident commissioner was appointed in 1904. A council of islanders was established first, then replaced by an elected assembly in 1960. The island became independent in 1974.

Niue is self-governing, in free association with New Zealand. All Niueans have New Zealand citizenship.

Most of Niue's agricultural products are consumed on the island. The country is working to develop a stronger tourist trade and to augment its growing financial services industry. Its economy is heavily dependent on foreign aid, most of which comes from New Zealand.

BRAND X PICTURES

Northern Marianas

COMMONWEALTH OF THE NORTHERN MARIANA ISLANDS

The Northern Marianas is a chain of sixteen coral and volcanic islands in the Pacific Ocean between the Philippines and Hawaii. Six of the island are inhabited. The principal islands are Rota, Tinian and Saipan. Saipan contains the seat of government, a busy seaport and an international airport. The climate is tropical with high temperatures throughout the year.

Only forty percent of the population was born in the Northern Marianas. Large numbers of guest workers, notably from the Philippines, are employed in the garment industry. The indigenous people are United States citizens. Christianity is the dominant religion. English, Chamorro and Carolinian are the most commonly used languages.

The islands were inhabited as early as 1500 B.C. Spanish explorer Ferdinand Magellan was the first European to arrive there in A.D. 1521. He named the islands the Ladrones (Thieves Islands). Jesuit priests arrived in 1668 to establish missions. The islands were renamed the Marianas for Mariana of Austria, then regent of Spain. The islands, which then included Guam, became a Spanish possession. The Spanish paid little attention to them.

Control of Guam went to the United States following the Spanish American War of 1898.

The other islands were sold to Germany. Japan occupied the Marianas following the outbreak of war in Europe in 1914. It retained control from 1920 under a mandate from the League of Nations.

Japan established military bases on the islands during the 1930s. Those on Tinian and Saipan came under massive attack from Allied forces during World War II. Many people on both sides were killed.

The islands were made a part of the U.S.-administered UN Trust Territory of the Pacific Islands in 1947. The residents voted to become an independent commonwealth within the United States in 1975. They became U.S. citizens in 1986. The UN Security Council formally ended its trusteeship in 1990.

The economy of the Marianas is based on garment manufacturing, agriculture and tourism. Major exports include clothing and other manufactured goods. The 1976 Northern Marianas Convenant with the U.S. government set its minimum wage for workers lower than that of the U.S. The islands are also exempt from U.S. immigration and import laws. These conditions have fostered a rapid growth in the garment industry. Laborers are imported to work under what some critics have described as sweatshop conditions.

GOVERNMENT
Website www.mariana-islands.gov.mp
Capital Saipan
Type of government
Self-governing commonwealth, associated with USA
Voting Universal adult suffrage
Head of state President of the USA
Head of government Governor
Constitution 1901
Legislature
Bicameral Congress
House of Representatives (lower house), Senate (upper house)
Judiciary
Commonwealth Supreme Court

LAND AND PEOPLE
Land area 189 sq mi (490 sq km)
Highest point
3,166 ft (965 m)
Coastline 921 mi (1,482 km)
Population 77,311
Ethnic groups
Filipino 33%, Chamorro 24%, Chinese 11%, Carolinian 10%
Religions Christianity 80%
Languages
English, Chamorro, Carolinian

ECONOMIC
Currency US dollar
Industry
tourism, garments, handicrafts
Agriculture
coconuts, fruits, vegetables, cattle
Natural resources
seafood

Norway

KINGDOM OF NORWAY

A traditionally dressed Norwegian woman stands before a backdrop of spectacular scenery.

BRAND X PICTURES

GOVERNMENT
Website odin.dep.no
Capital Oslo
Type of government
Constitutional monarchy
Independence from Sweden
June 7,1905
Voting Universal adult suffrage
Head of state Monarch
Head of government Prime
Minister
Constitution 1814
Legislature
Unicameral Parliament (Storting)
Judiciary Supreme Court
Member of CE, IMF, NATO, OECD,
UN, UNESCO, UNHCR, WHO, WTO

LAND AND PEOPLE
Land area 125,050 sq mi
(323,878 sq km)
Highest point Glittertinden
8,100 ft (2,472 m)
Coastline 13,200 mi (21,200 km)
Population 4,503,440
Major cities and populations
Oslo 505,000
Bergen 230,000
Trondheim 150,000
Ethnic groups
Scandinavian 97%
Religion Christianity
Languages Norwegian (official),
indigenous languages

ECONOMIC
Currency Krone
Industry
petroleum, gas, food processing,
shipbuilding, paper products,
metals, chemicals, timber, mining,
textiles, fishing
Agriculture
barley, wheat, potatoes, pork, beef,
veal, milk
Natural resources
petroleum, copper, natural gas,
pyrites, nickel, iron ore, zinc, lead,
seafood, timber

Norway occupies the western and northern portions of the Scandinavian peninsula in northwestern Europe. Its long coastline features majestically beautiful fjords and offshore islands formed by glacial movement over millions of years. The inland areas are dominated by rugged mountains and high plateaus. Norway has many thousands of glacial lakes, the largest of which is Mjosa, in the southeast. Most of the country's fertile land is found in the valleys of the fjords on the western coast. About one third of the country is heavily forested.

Northern Norway experiences Arctic conditions during winter. There are freezing winds and heavy snowfalls. The southern climate is more moderate, although still cool to cold in winter. Coastal areas are affected by the Gulf Stream, which provides warmer temperatures.

All but three percent of Norwegians are descended from people of Scandinavian backgrounds. One noteworthy exception is a small community of Lapp people in the far north. Norway is a Christian country. Ninety-five percent of the people are adherents of Norway's Evangelical Lutheran Church. Norwegian is the official language. Lappish and Finnish speakers can be found in the far northern regions.

The electrochemical and electrometallurgical industries form the most important parts of the country's manufacturing. Shipbuilding continues to be a major industry as well. Other manufactured products include machinery, pulp and paper goods, textiles and processed foods.

Offshore petroleum drilling began in the 1970s. Oil exports, as well as those of natural gas, have grown considerably since that time. There is intensive

Norway

mining of titanium, copper and iron ore. The rugged landscape is ideal for generating hydro-electric power for export as well as domestic use.

Forestry accounts for a small part of the annual gross national product. Most wood products are harvested in the south and east. Less than 3% of Norway's land is suitable for farming. Agriculture is not a major part of its economy.

Norway is one of world's leading suppliers of fish. Herring, mackerel and cod are harvested from the surrounding oceans. They are exported in fresh, canned or salted condition to many parts of the world.

Norway is a constitutional monarchy. The role of the hereditary monarch is purely ceremonial. Political power resides with the cabinet of ministers headed by the prime minister. The council is formed with the support of members of the parliament, called the Storting. It is unicameral, with members elected for fixed four-year terms. There are nineteen provinces, called fylkers, each with its own local assembly.

Norway was inhabited as early as 14,000 years ago by hunting people who came from western and central Europe. There were some 29 kingdoms in Scandinavia by the eighth century A.D. Norse warriors raided much of western Europe, beginning in the ninth

century. They established the Norse duchy of Normandy on the French coast.

The first successful attempt at forming a united kingdom of all the minor Norse holdings was achieved by King Harald I in the ninth century. He had established control over all of Norway by 900. He also conquered the Orkney and Shetland Islands off the coast of Scotland. Christianity was introduced after 1015, during the reign of Olaf II.

Many nobles were unhappy with the rule of the monarchs. They joined forces with King Canute of England and Denmark, who invaded Norway and deposed Olaf II in 1028. The ensuing dispute over royal succession began a civil war.

Norway went into decline for many decades. Eventually it stabilized under the rule of King Sverre beginning in 1184. His successors, Haakon IV and Magnus VI, built on his efforts. They began considerable social and economic advancements. Norway, Sweden and Denmark were briefly united under one crown by the end of the fourteenth century.

The bubonic plague, popularly known as the Black Death, swept Norway in 1349. It claimed the lives of more than sixty percent of the people. Norway was ruled by governors appointed from Copenhagen, Denmark until

the nineteenth century. Much of the commerce was controlled by merchants of the Germanic Hanseatic League.

Swedish attempts to gain control of Norway in the early eighteenth century were thwarted by the Danish navy. Denmark was allied with France during the Napoleonic Wars. Norway was forced to participate on Denmark's behalf. British warships blockaded Norwegian ports.

The Napoleonic Wars at the beginning of the nineteenth century brought an end to the union. The Treaty of Kiel forced Denmark to cede Norway to Sweden in 1814. Norwegian resistance was formidable. Sweden was forced to recognize a separate Norwegian parliament with considerable autonomy in internal affairs. Norway experienced healthy economic, political and artistic growth for the rest of the nineteenth century.

Norway moved to establish its own diplomatic representation in other countries during the early 1900s. Sweden opposed this. The Norwegian parliament declared that Sweden's King Oscar II was no longer ruler of Norway. The Norwegian people voted overwhelmingly for separation from Sweden in 1905. Sweden ratified the separation. Prince Carl of Denmark became Norway's King Haakon VII.

The liberal Norwegian government was soon well-known for its landmark legislation. It led Europe in employment benefits and laws regarding divorce. It granted women the right to vote in 1913.

Several Norwegians soon won international acclaim. Painter Edvard Munch, composer Edvard Grieg and playwright Henrik Ibsen produced important works. Explorer Roald Amundsen was first to reach the South Pole in 1902.

Norway experienced an economic boom during World War I, during which it remained neutral. The 1920s was a period of large-scale industrialization, aided by the development of hydroelectric power. The Labor Party came to power in 1927 and launched a series of radical social measures. Public health services, public housing, aid for the disabled and enlarged pensions were all introduced.

Norway again declared itself neutral in World War II. Germany invaded in 1940, attacking all of its major ports. The king and his ministers fled to London, where they established a government-in-exile.

Pro-Nazi fascists led by Vidkun Quisling collaborated with the Germans. Norwegians quickly formed resistance movements. They maintained a guerrilla war against German forces until liberation in 1945.

Norway was a founding member of the United Nations. Norwegian Trygve Lie was its first secretary-general. Norway joined NATO in 1949 and was co-founder of the European Free Trade Association in 1960. Norwegians voted against membership in the European Economic Community (later the European Union) in 1972. They reaffirmed this decision in 1994.

Norway contributed substantially to peace in the Middle East in 1993. It sponsored discussions between Yasir Arafat's Palestine Liberation Organization and the Israeli government for development of a program for Palestinian self-rule.

Norway's constant refusal to abide by International Whaling Commission regulations has affected its reputation among animal rights advocates. It led a group of nations which blocked the establishment of a Pacific Ocean whale sanctuary in 2000.

Timber wharves and warehouses at Trondheim.

Oman

SULTANATE OF OMAN

Oman is located along the southeastern coast of the Arabian Peninsula. The coastal plain on the Gulf of Oman coast is known as al-Batinah. Most farming is done in this area. The Green-Mountains are a barrier between coast and the desert. The country also includes a northern tip of the peninsula, separated from the rest of Oman by the United Arab Emirates. The average temperatures is 83°F (28.3°C). Rainfall is sparse, except on the coast.

Arabs make up most of Oman's population. Three-quarters of the people are Ibadi Muslims. Smaller numbers are Sunnis and Shi'ites. There is a small Hindu community. Arabic is the official language.

An Arab chief from Hira in Mesopotamia founded a kingdom in Oman in the third century A.D. The Omanis accepted Islam in the seventh century and elected their first imam (religious leader) in 751. The Qarmations conquered the country in the tenth century.

The Portuguese were the first Europeans to arrive, in 1507. They captured Masqat for a trading post. The Portugese were driven out in 1650.

Ahmed bin Said expelled Iranians who had gained a major presence by 1741. He went on to found the dynastry which is still in power today. Its ruler later became known as sultan.

The Ibadis, who wanted a dynasty ruled by Islam, declared an independent state in the 1920s. Their rebellion was assisted by Saudi Arabia. The government suppressed them with British help. A second major rebellion occurred in the 1950s. It was also squelched with British aid.

Sultan Said bin Taimur was deposed by his son Qabus in 1970. Muscat and Oman became the Sultanate of Oman. Oil revenues were used to facilitate social change and economic development. Fear of Soviet invasion prompted the sultan to seek a promise of U.S. military assistance. In exchange, the U.S. was allowed access to Oman's military bases. Oman cooperated with the allied forces against Iraq in the Persian Gulf War.

The sultan ruled with absolute authority, with no constitution or formal legal system until 1996. Qabus established a popularly elected National Assembly in 1997, although he held a veto over who could serve in the legislature. Privatization of industries in the 1990s generated unemployment and widespread protests. Oman allowed its bases to be used by British and American forces after the September 11, 2001 attacks on the U.S. prompted a search for al-Qaeda members in

GOVERNMENT
Website www.omanet.com
Capital Muscat
Type of government Monarchy
Voting Limited to small number of voters chosen by the government
Head of state Sultan
Head of government Sultan
Constitution none
Legislature Bicameral Parliament (Majlis Oman)
Majlis al-Shura (lower house), Majlis al-Dawla (upper house)
Judiciary Supreme Court
Member of AL, IMF, UN, UNESCO, WHO, WTO

LAND AND PEOPLE
Land area 82,030 sq mi (212,450 sq km)
Highest point Jabal Shams 9,777 ft (2,980 m)
Coastline 1,300 mi (2092 km)
Population 2,622,200
Major cities and populations Muscat 500,000
Ethnic groups Arab 95%, others 5%
Religions Islam 98%, Hinduism 2%
Languages Arabic (official)

ECONOMIC
Currency Omani rial
Industry oil production, oil refining, natural gas production, cement, mining
Agriculture dates, limes, bananas, alfalfa, vegetables, livestock
Natural resources petroleum, copper, asbestos, limestone, chromium, gypsum, natural gas

Pakistan

ISLAMIC REPUBLIC OF PAKISTAN

GOVERNMENT
Website www.pakistan.gov.pk
Capital Islamabad
Type of government
Interim military regime
Independence from Britain
August 15, 1947 (dominion status)
Voting Universal adult suffrage
Head of state and government
Chief of Army Staff
Constitution 1973, suspended
1999
Legislature
Bicameral Parliament (suspended)
National Assembly (lower house),
Senate (upper house)
Judiciary Supreme Court
Member of CN (suspended), IMF,
UN, UNESCO, UNHCR, WHO, WTO

LAND AND PEOPLE
Land area 307,373 sq mi
(796,095 sq km)
Highest point Mt. Godwin-Austen
28,251 ft (8,611 m)
Coastline 650 mi (1,046 km)
Population 144,616,639
Major cities and populations
Karachi 12 million
Lahore 6 million
Faisalabad 2.2 million
Ethnic groups
Punjabi 55%, Pashtun 13%
Religions
Islam 97%, Hinduism 1%
Languages Urdu, English (both
official), indigenous languages

ECONOMIC
Currency Rupee
Industry
textiles, food processing, beverages,
construction materials, clothing,
paper products, mining
Agriculture
cotton, wheat, rice, sugar cane,
fruits, vegetables dairy, beef,
mutton
Natural resources
natural gas, petroleum, low-quality
coal, iron ore, copper, salt,
limestone

Pakistan is in the northwestern corner of the Indian sub-continent of Asia. The Indus River separates the Indus Plain and the Baluchistan Highlands. The river runs the length of the country, opening to a vast and very fertile flood plain near the coast. Part of the Himalaya Mountains crosses the north. The Thar Desert covers the border with India in the southeast.

The mountainous north is extremely cold. Lower lying regions tend to be cool in winter and warm to hot in summer. Heat and humidity increase markedly near the coastline. The heaviest rains fall along the Indus Valley and on the coast.

The largest ethnic group is the Punjabi, most of whom live in the northeast. The estimated three million Afghan refugees have decreased somewhat since the fall of the Taliban regime in Afghanistan.

All but three percent of the population is Muslim. Twenty percent are Shi'ite, the rest Sunni. Hindus make up the largest religious minority. The official languages are Urdu and English. About half of the people speak Punjabi. Other languages are Sindhi, Pashto and Baluchi.

Agriculture is Pakistan's key industry. Most farming is done in the fertile Indus Valley. Pakistan has the world's largest irrigation system, supporting its massive cotton growing and export program. Oil refining and metal processing are also substantial industries.

Pakistan exports people in large numbers to work as laborers and domestic servants, particularly to Middle Eastern countries. Their earnings represent major revenue.

Pakistan is officially a parliamentary republic. However, the constitution was suspended following a military coup in October 1999. The constitution adopted in 1973 was amended in 1985. The parliament was bicameral. The National Assembly, or lower house, was elected by the people. The Sen-

FLAT EARTH PICTURE GALLERY

Pakistan

The spectacular Hindu Kush region of Pakistan.

FLAT EARTH PICTURE GALLERY

ate, or upper house, was elected by provincial assemblies. The prime minister was head of government. The president, as head of state, was elected for five years by the parliament and provincial assemblies.

The present ruling body is the National Security Council. It is made up of army, navy and air force chiefs and four civilians.

Tiny agricultural villages grew up in the area of Pakistan, evolving into larger centers around 3500 B.C. A cohesive civilization had developed along the Indus valley during the next 1,000 years. Indo-Aryans invaded the region around 1500 B.C. The Indus civilization began its decline.

The Persian Empire gained control of the region around 500 B.C. The area was con-

quered by Alexander the Great in 326 B.C. Following the breakup of his empire, the Seleucids ruled briefly until displaced by the Mauryas.

Over the next 400 years control passed from the Mauryas to the Bactrians to the Saka. It was then conquered by the Parthians followed by the Kushans. A Kushan leader, Kanishka, controlled most of today's Pakistan from a capital at Peshawar.

Arab forces, commanded by Muhammad bin Qasim, conquered the Sind region in A.D. 712. They introduced Islam and Sharia (Islamic law). Muslim conquests extended across the Indian sub-continent as far as Bengal in the following centuries.

The Muslim Mogul Empire of the seventeenth and eighteenth centuries includes most

of present-day Pakistan, India and Bangladesh. Sikh kingdoms gained power within the empire during the early 1800s.

European traders had competed for power within the region beginning in the fifteenth century. The British East India Company became the strongest European force by the eighteenth century. The breakup of the Mogul Empire in the 1740s brought increasing power to that company.

The British East India Company gained control of Sind in 1843 and Punjab in 1849. After the 1857 Indian revolt, control of the region passed to the government of Britain. Political reforms were made. The Indian National Congress, representing the Hindu majority, was created in 1885.

Britain failed to subdue the Pathan in the northwest. Britain established the North-West Frontier province in 1901 to satisfy these people. Much of the balance of Pakistan was included in British India at this time.

Two major religious groups, the Muslims and the Hindus, dominated India. There was little interaction, despite efforts of the Hindu-based Indian National Congress to include Muslims in its ranks. The concept of Muslims as a separate

12

political entity was encouraged by the British, with electorates based on religion.

Formation of the Muslim League in 1906 led to greater tension between Muslims and Hindus. The poet Muhammad Iqbal began a movement for a separate Muslim state in 1930. It would be called Pakistan, from the Urdu words Pak for pure, Stan for land.

Muslim League leader Muhammad Ali Jinnah formally demanded separate states wherever Muslims were in the majority in 1940. Britain proposed an Indian federation with separately governed religiously based provinces. The Muslim League refused.

Britain announced the subcontinent would be partitioned geographically. The northwestern Indus Valley region would become Muslim Pakistan. The east would be Muslim East Bengal. Hindu India would occupy the center. India and Pakistan would become British dominions. The British monarch would be the head of state.

Millions of Muslims moved from their lifetime homes to the new Muslim nation. Similarly, Hindus departed for India. Tension between Muslim and Hindu exploded into warfare. Widespread massacres took one-half million lives.

The Muslim League's Jinnah was governor-general of Pakistan and Liaqat Ali Khan was prime minister. Karachi was its capital. Ownership of Kashmir, in the far northwest, was disputed between Pakistan and India. The matter remains unresolved today.

Jinnah died in 1948. Liaqat Ali Khan was assassinated three years later by an Afghan fanatic. Years of political instability and economic problems provoked a state of emergency in 1954. East Bengal was renamed East Pakistan. Pakistan ended dominion status. It became a republic under its constitution of 1955.

Administration of two widely separated territories proved difficult. President Mirza had to impose martial law in 1958. General Muhammad Ayub Khan became prime minister and was elected president in 1960. He created an Islamic republic with two languages, Bengali in the east, Urdu in the west. Construction of a new capital city began at Islamabad.

Failure to solve the Kashmir problem led to warfare between Pakistan and India in April 1965. The United States suspended military and economic aid to both countries. The Soviet Union mediated the conflict. It ended with the Declaration of Tashkent the same year.

Ayub Khan resigned in March 1970 following unrest in East Pakistan over control from the west. The new leader, General Agha Muhammad Yahya Khan, immediately declared martial law.

The Awami League won overwhelming support in parliamentary elections in East Pakistan. Yahya Khan postponed the convening of parliament and imprisoned the Awami League leader. East Pakistan declared itself independent in 1971, calling itself Bangladesh.

The Pakistani army, composed entirely of West Pakistanis, occupied Bangladesh. War erupted and hundreds of thousands died. Ten million people fled to India. Indian troops intervened in December of

The bustle of a Karachi bus station.

Pakistan

1971. Pakistan surrendered after two weeks of fighting.

Yahya Khan acknowledged the presidency of Zulfikar Ali Bhutto, leader of the Pakistan People's Party on December 20, 1971. Bhutto immediately began nationaling key industries and financial institutions. This move led to severe inflation and growing unrest in urban areas.

General Zia ul-Haq deposed Bhutto in 1977. Martial law was imposed once again. Zia assumed the presidency the following year. He established Sharia as the law of the land.

Zia died suspiciously in a 1988 plane crash. Benazir Bhutto, daughter of the former leader, was elected prime minister the following November. She was the first woman to lead an Islamic country. President Ghulam Ishaq Khan dismissed Bhutto in 1990, charging her with abuse of power.

Nawaz Sharif was elected prime minister. He too was dismissed when he sought to reduce presidential powers in 1993. Bhutto regained the prime ministership until 1996 when she was again dismissed, this time on charges of corruption.

Nawaz Sharif was returned to power with a huge majority in the 1997 elections. He passed legislation banning heads of state from dismissing elected governments. The president was forced to resign.

India conducted a nuclear weapons test in May 1998. Pakistan responded with a similar test. The U.S. imposed economic sanctions on both countries.

Prime Minister Sharif blocked an aircraft carrying military leader General Pervez Musharraf from landing in Pakistan during a military coup in 1999. Musharraf had Sharif convicted of hijacking an aircraft. Sharif was exiled to Saudi Arabia in 2000. Musharaff appointed himself president in June 2001.

Following the September 2001 terrorist attacks in New York and Washington, D.C., the U.S. dropped sanctions against Pakistan in return for support in toppling the Taliban government in Afghanistan. Pakistan agreed to allow the U.S. to use its military facilities in that operation. Pakistan had previously supported the Taliban.

India threatened war when guerillas killed 40 people at its summer capital in India-held Kashmir in 2001. Another 14 people were killed in a similar attack two months later. Musharraf took steps to curb the activities of radical groups.

Musharaff held a referendum, seeking voters' permission to remain in office for another five years, in April of 2002. He declared victory. The following month, Islamic terrorist killed 34 people in India-held Kashmir. Musharaff vowed to find a permanent end to terrorist activities. A bomb near the U.S. consulate in Karachi killed 12 people and injured 50 others on June 14th.

A heavily loaded vehicle crosses a stream in rural Pakistan.

Palau

REPUBLIC OF PALAU

GOVERNMENT
Capital Koror
Type of government
Republic, in free association with USA
Independence from designation as UN Trust Territory
October 1, 1994
Voting Universal adult suffrage
Head of state President
Head of government President
Constitution 1981
Legislature
Bicameral Congress (Olbiil Era Kelulau)
House of Delegates (lower house), Senate (upper house)
Judiciary Supreme Court
Member of
IMF, SPF, UN, UNESCO, WHO, WTO

LAND AND PEOPLE
Land area 188 sq mi (487 sq km)
Highest point
Mount Ngerchelchuus
794 ft (242 m)
Coastline
944 mi (1,519 km)
Population 19,092
Major cities and populations
Koror 30,300
Ethnic groups
Mixed Polynesian, Melanesian, Malay
Religion Christianity
Languages
English, Palauan (both official)

ECONOMIC
Currency US dollar
Industry
tourism, handicraft, garments, mining
Agriculture coconuts, copra, tapioca, sweet potatoes
Natural resources
forests, gold, seafood, seabed minerals

Palau is an archipelago of more than 200 islands, islets and atolls of the Carolines chain in the western Pacific Ocean. Many of the islands are fringed by coral reefs. Some of the islands are low-lying, others feature mountainous terrain. The climate is tropical with a rainy season from May to November.

The major islands include Koror, the current seat of the government. Babelthuap is the planned site of the future capital.

Palauans have mixed Polynesian, Melanesian and Malay backgrounds. There is a significant guest worker community, most of whom are Filipinos and Chinese. Most Palauans are Christians. Palauan and English are the official languages.

The leading occupations of Palau include fishing and agriculture. The country relies on aid from the United States.

The first Palauans were migrants from Southeast Asia around 1000 B.C. They were subsequently joined by Polynesian and Melanesian peoples. Spain exercised loose control from the seventeenth century onwards. It made no real effort to exploit the Carolines, as they had been named.

Europeans established trading posts in the nineteenth century. Whaling ships made regular calls. Missionaries were successful in converting indigenous peoples to Christianity. Many indigenous people died from diseases brought to the islands by the Europeans.

Spain sold the Carolines to Germany following the 1898 Spanish American War. Japan occupied the Carolines in 1914. Following World War I, in 1920, the League of Nations gave Japan a mandate over the Carolines.

Many Japanese migrated to the islands to develop business enterprises. Japan constructed military facilities in the Carolines after its withdrawal from the League of Nations in 1935. Palau was the scene of numerous major battles between Allied forces and the Japanese during World War II.

The islands became a United Nations trust territory administered by the United States in 1947. Palauans rejected a United States' proposal for a single Micronesian federation in the 1970s.

The islands adopted a republican constitution in 1980. A compact of free association with the United States was signed. The U.S. accepted responsibility for defense of the islands.

Palau became independent in 1994. It was the last of the United Nations trust territories. Palau joined the United Nations the same year. It then became an African, Caribbean and Pacific (ACP) state of the European Union.

Panama

Panama is located on the isthmus liking South America with Central America. The country is bounded on the north by the Caribbean Sea, on the east by Colombia and on the south by the Pacific Ocean. It is bisected by the Panama Canal. Two moutain ranges cross much of the country. A region of hilly forests with plains and high plateaus falls between those ranges. Panama's tropical climate features consistently high temperatures and humidity all year long, with a dry season between January and April.

Seventy percent of the population are mestizos, descended from both European and indigenous peoples. There is a significant African minority descended from the canal builders. Most of the population is Christian. Spanish is the official language.

Panama was part of Colombia until the early twentieth century. Indigenous peoples inhabited the region when Spaniard Rodrigo de Bastidas arrived in 1501. The first successful Spanish settlement was made by explorer Diego de Niscuesa in 1508. The indigenous population was wiped out by forced labor or introduced diseases within a short time.

Explorer Vasco Núñez de Balboa sighted the Pacific in 1513. He realized that the relatively short voyage across the isthmus from the Caribbean to the Pacific could cut months off sailing time around Cape Horn. Cargo from the Spanish Philippines could be unloaded from ships on the Pacific coast. Goods could be carried across the strip of land, then reloaded on another ship in the Caribbean.

Panama was made a part of the viceroyalty of New Granada, a Spanish holding. The isthmus became a popular route for traffic to and from Peru. Panama declared itself indpendent from Spain in 1821. It voluntarily became part of Colombia.

Gold prospectors rushing to reach the west coast of the United States in the mid-1800s used the Panama land crossing in large numbers. An American company was granted rights to build the coast-to-coast Panama Railroad, which was completed in 1855.

French interests began construction of a ship canal through Panama in 1881. Mismanagement and disease among the workers caused the project to fail. The United States was intent on seeing the canal completed. Nicaragua had been the favored site until the French company offered its Panama rights to the United States.

The Colombian legislature failed to ratify an agreement with the United States concerning the canal in 1903. Panama declared its independence, which was immediately recognized by the U.S.

A treaty was signed with the new government of Panama, giving the United States the

A cruise liner passing through Gatun Lock in the Panama Canal.

LONELY PLANET IMAGES – ALFREDO MAIQUEZ

BRAND X PICTURES

The skyline of Panama City.

right to dig the canal and occupy and control a strip of land on either side. The U.S. paid Panama $10 million and agreed to pay $250,000 each year after. It also guaranteed Panama's independence and gained the right to intervene in the case of military problems in the country.

The canal opened on August 15, 1914. The United States maintained total control of the Panama Canal Zone. American forces were sent to restore order in Panama in 1908, 1912 and 1918. As anti-U.S. sentiment grew, the right to intervene was revoked in 1936.

Military coups occurred in 1941, 1949 and 1951. The National Guard, led by Colonel Omar Torrijos Herrera, deposed

the elected president in 1968. He abolished political parties and introduced major land reform. A treaty with the United States in the late 1970s set a 1999 date for Panama's takeover of the Canal Zone.

General Manuel Antonio Noriega took control of the country through a series of puppet presidents beginning in 1983. Noriega was accused of drug trafficking in 1987. The United States imposed stringent sanctions and political pressure intended to help remove Noreiga from power. Guilllermo Endara was elected president in 1989, but Noreiga nullified the vote.

Noreiga suppressed a military coup in October of the same year. United States forces invaded in November. Endara was installed as president. The 25,000 American troops were victorious in early 1990, despite considerable opposition. Noriega was indicted on drug trafficking charges in 1992.

United States military forces withdrew from the Panama Canal Zone in September of 1997. The canal was formally handed over to Panama on December 31, 1999. Panama's first woman president, Mireya Elisa Moscoso, had been elected president earlier in the year.

GOVERNMENT
Capital Panama City
Type of government Republic
Separation from Colombia
November 3, 1903
Voting
Universal adult suffrage, compulsory
Head of state President
Head of government President
Constitution 1972
Legislature
Bicameral Parliament
House of Representatives (lower house), Senate (upper house)
Judiciary Supreme Court
Member of IMF, OAS, UN, UNESCO, WHO, WTO

LAND AND PEOPLE
Land area
29,762 sq mi (77,082 sq km)
Highest point
Volcan de Chiriqui
11,400 ft (3,475 m)
Coastline 1,547 mi (2,490 km)
Population 2,845,647
Major cities and populations
Panama City 1.1 million
San Miguelito 294,000
Ethnic groups
Mestizo 70%, African 14%, European 10%, indigenous 6%
Religion Christianity 99%
Languages Spanish (official), English, indigenous languages

ECONOMIC
Currency Balboa
Industry
shipping services, petroleum refining, brewing, cement, sugar milling
Agriculture
bananas, rice, corn, coffee, sugar cane, vegetables, livestock, seafood
Natural resources
copper, mahogany forests, seafood

Papua New Guinea

INDEPENDENT STATE OF PAPUA NEW GUINEA

Papua New Guinea is a collection of 600 islands immediately north of Australia in the western Pacific Ocean. It occupies the eastern half of New Guinea island as well as the other primary islands of Bougainville, Buka and Woodlark. The mainland is dominated by the rugged mountain ranges. Thick rainforests cover most of the remaining landscape. High temperatures and humidity persist throughout the year.

The majority of the people are native Papuans. The numerous tribal groups are Melanesian. Christianity is the dominant religion, but a small percentage of the people practice animism. English, Pidgin and Motu are the official languages. There are at least 750 indigenous languages.

Asian peoples migrated to Papua New Guinea from Asia thousands of years ago. Spanish explorer Jorge de Menezes was the first European to land on the islands in A.D. 1527. The Spanish named the mainland New Guinea. The British East India Company claimed the entire island in 1793. The Netherlands disputed the claim, taking possession of the western half in 1828.

Germany annexed the northeastern portion of the island, calling it Kaiser Wilhelmsland in 1884. Panic in Australia led the colony of Queensland to annex the southeastern portion for Britain.

British New Guinea was transferred to Australia in 1906 as the Territory of Papua. Australian troops seized German New Guinea in 1914. It was officially mandated to Australia by the League of Nations in 1920.

Japan occupied some of the smaller islands and the northern half of the mainland during World War II. A large Japanese force occupied New Guinea until the war ended.

The Territory of Papua and New Guinea was made a UN trust territory in 1949, with Australia as administrative power. The Netherlands gave up control of the western half in 1962. It is now a province of Indonesia. Papua New Guinea became independent on September 16, 1975.

A revolt against the management of a major copper mine led the Bougainville Revolutionary Army to declare independence of that island in 1990. The government launched offensives against the rebels until a 1997 cease-fire agreement was signed.

The country suffered serious drought in the late 1990s. At least 2,000 people died when a tsunami devastated the northwestern coast in 1998. These events, as well as the effects of the revolution and unstable governments, have left the economy in dire condition.

GOVERNMENT
Website www.pngonline.gov.pg
Capital Port Moresby
Type of government
Constitutional monarchy
Independence from Australia
September 16, 1975
Voting Universal adult suffrage
Head of state
British Crown,
represented by Governor-General
Head of government Prime Minister
Constitution 1975
Legislature
Unicameral National Parliament
Judiciary Supreme Court
Member of APEC, CN, IMF, SPF, UN, UNESCO, WHO, WTO

LAND AND PEOPLE
Land area 178,704 sq mi
(462,840 sq km)
Highest point Mt. Wilhelm
14,793 ft (4,509 m)
Coastline 3,210 mi (5,152 km)
Population 5,049,055
Major cities and populations
Port Moresby 220,000
Lae 113,000
Madang 32,000
Ethnic groups
Papuan 84%, Melanesian 15%
Religions
Christianity, traditional indigenous
Languages
English, Tok Pisin, Motu (all official), several indigenous dialects

ECONOMIC
Currency Kina
Industry
copra crushing, palm oil processing, wood production, mining, crude oil production
Agriculture
coffee, cacao, coconuts, palm kernels, tea, rubber, sweet potatoes, fruit, vegetables, poultry, pigs
Natural resources
gold, copper, silver, natural gas, timber, oil, seafood

Paraguay

REPUBLIC OF PARAGUAY

Paraguay is a landlocked country in central South America between Brazil and Argentina. The Paraguay River flows from north to south, creating Paraguay's Región Occidental in the west and Región Oriental in the east. The east is fertile, while the west is arid. The climate is subtropical with cool to warm winters and warm to hot summers.

All but five percent of Paraguay's people are mestizos, of a mixed Spanish and Gaurani descent. Minorities of indigenous peoples, Asians, Europeans and others make up the balance. There is also a German-Canadian Mennonite community in Chaco and a small group of Japanese in the Región Occidental. Paraguay is almost completely Christian. Spanish is the official language, but almost all of the population speak Gaurani.

The region that is now Paraguay was inhabited for centuries by the Gaurani people. The Spanish and the Portugese explored the area in the early sixteenth century. Adventurers seeking gold established a fort on the Paraguay River in 1537. Colonial Paraguay and the territory of present-day Argentina were jointly ruled until 1620, when they became part of the viceroyalty of Peru.

Jesuit missionaries established strong communities in the south-east during the seventeenth and early eighteenth centuries. Spanish administrators expelled them in 1767, leaving the indigenous population at the mercy of slave traders.

Spain created the viceroyalty of La Plata in 1776. It included Argentina, Paraguay, Uruguay and Peru. Argentina declared its independence in 1810. Paraguay proclaimed its own independence on May 14, 1811. For two years Argentina tried without success to annex Paraguay.

José Gaspar Rodríguez became dictator of Paraguay in 1814. Paraguay prospered under his authoritarian rule. He stripped the church of its powers and broke the power of elite land-owners. When he died in 1840,

Buskers and street stalls in Encarnacion in eastern Paraguay.

FLAT EARTH PICTURE GALLERS

Paraguay

Rodriguez was succeeded by Carlos Antonio López, who ruled with the same powers until 1862.

Paraguay's third dictator, López's son Francisco Solano, was not a good leader. He wanted to build a large empire, so he launched a war against the alliance of Urugay, Brazil and Argentina in 1865. His death in 1870 ended the conflict. More than half of the country's people had been killed. The economy was destroyed and agriculture had been all but halted.

The effects of the war were felt for decades. No president was allowed to serve a full term until 1912. A series of strong leaders held office until the late 1920s, enabling Paraguay to gain some peace and prosperity.

The border with Bolivia was the scene of many incidents from 1929 to 1932. A full-scale war was fought until a peace was reached in 1935. The government was restructured after the war to permit widespread economic and social reforms. The constitution of 1940 gave the state tight reins on all economic activity. Paraguay fought for the Allied powers in World War II. It was a charter member of the United Nations.

General Higino Morínigo held power from 1940 to 1948. His was an authoritarian dictatorship regularly challenged by uprisings. Paraguay had six different presidents between 1948 and 1954. This instability ended when the army staged a coup, bringing General Alfredo Stroessner to the presidency.

Stroessner provided strong national leadership. The economy improved. He established close economic relations with neighboring countries. Foreign ministers from Argentina, Bolivia, Brazil, Paraguay and Uruguay signed the La Plata Basin Pact. It was designed to develop the La Plata River Basin, much to the benefit of Paraguay.

Stroessner's party won the next eight elections. Many people had grown tired of authoritarianism and repression by the late 1980s. General Andres Rodriguez led a coup, sending Stroessner into exile in 1989.

Rodriguez won a subsequent election and vowed to give up the office to a civilian by 1993. He constructed a democratic institution previously unknown to Paraguayans. Juan Carlos Wasmosy won the presidency in 1993, following constitutional revisions.

Several political upheavals have occurred since that time. Violent protests, coups d'etat, assassinations and scandals have become commonplace. Extremely weak economic conditions continue to threaten the country's fragile democracy.

Rodriguez was convicted of corruption in 2002. President Raúl Cubas Grau was impeached for misuse of public office in mid-1999. He returned from exile in Brazil in 2002 to answer charges of complicity in the assassination of his deputy. An attempted coup by supporters of Lino Oviedo in May 2000 was a failure.

Grain silos in rural Paraguay.

Peru

REPUBLIC OF PERU

Peru lies on the northwestern coast of South America. Most of the population lives on its coastal plain. The climate is arid and the land is not particularly fertile. The landscape rises from the coast to form the Cordillera Occidental mountain range. The Cordillera Oriental range lies to the east. Both ranges are crossed by numerous rivers, creating deep valleys and fertile agricultural land. Much of the land beyond the Cordillera Oriental is rainforest.

Climatic conditions vary greatly across Peru. The coastal plains are cool to warm in winter and hot in summer. Winters in the mountains are cold, and summers cool to mild. Temperatures and humidity are consistently high in the eastern rainforests.

Half of Peru's population are indigenous peoples. About thirty five percent are mestizos, with mixed European and indigenous backgrounds. The European population is just over ten percent of the total. There are also significant African, Japanese and Chinese minorities. Most Peruvians are Catholic. Spanish and Quechua are the official languages.

Agriculture makes up a large part of Peru's economy. Crops include sugar cane, coffee, wheat, cotton, corn, barley and rice. Peru is the world's largest producer of the coca leaf, from which the drug cocaine is refined. Peruvian farmers raise many different kinds of livestock.

Fishing is also an important industry. More than forty percent of the catch is anchovies, used for making fish meal, a product in which Peru leads the world.

Peru is one of the world's leaders in the production of copper, silver, lead and zinc. Iron ore, gold, phosphate and coal are also mined. Oil is produced from wells on the coast and in the Amazon basin.

A colorful flower stall in a Lima market.

BRAND X PICTURES

GOVERNMENT
Capital Lima
Type of government Republic
Independence from Spain
July 28, 1821
Voting Universal adult suffrage
Head of state President
Head of government President
Constitution 1993
Legislature
Unicameral Congress of the Republic
Judiciary Supreme Court
Member of APEC, IMF, OAS, UN, UNESCO, WHO, WTO

LAND AND PEOPLE
Land area 496,225 sq mi
(1,285,216 sq km)
Highest point
Nevado Huascaran
22,205 ft (6,768 m)
Coastline
1,500 mi (2,414 km)
Population 27,483,864
Major cities and populations
Lima 7,443,000
Callao 650,000
Arequipa 710,103
Callao 424,294
Ethnic groups
Peruvians 45%, Mestizos 37%,
European 15%, others 3%
Religion Christianity
Languages
Quechua, English (both official)

ECONOMIC
Currency Nuevo sol
Industry
mining, petroleum, fishing, textiles, clothing, food processing, cement, motor vehicles, steel, shipbuilding
Agriculture
coffee, cotton, sugar cane, rice, wheat, potatoes, corn, coca, poultry, beef, dairy, wool
Natural resources
copper, silver, gold, petroleum, timber, seafood, iron ore, coal, phosphate, potash, natural gas

Peru

BRAND X PICTURES

Machu Picchu, the pinnacle of Inca civilization.

Manufacturing in Peru is done on a small scale compared to many other countries. Products include textiles, clothing, footwear, processed foods and electrical goods.

Inflation and a heavy debt slowed economic growth in the 1980s and the early 1990s. Considerable improvements have occurred since that time.

Peru's president, who is both head of state and head of government, is elected for a five-year term. The president is assisted by two vice-presidents and an appointed council of ministers. The members of the unicameral National Congress are elected for five years.

People lived in the region of Peru as early as 2000 B.C. Cultures such as the Chavin, Nazca and Chimu began to grow beginning around 1250 B.C.

The Inca civilization was on the rise by the twelfth century A.D. from its capital at Cuzco. It expanded from the Pacific Ocean east and from the region of modern Ecuador south to Chile by 1500. This vast empire was ruled by an Inca, or emperor, who was worshiped as a divinity. Its cultural excellence was typified by the magnificent city of Machu Picchu.

The extensive gold and silver deposits of the Inca realm attracted Spanish explorers. Spanish conquistadors led by Francisco Pizarro captured Inca leader Atahualpa in 1532. He was executed when he refused to accept Spanish control. The Inca empire declined rapidly.

Pizarro founded the city of Lima in 1535. It became the center of Spanish colonial rule. The conquistadors established

mines and large farms, forcing indigenous people to work under difficult conditions. Spain tried to put an end forced labor in 1544. The conquistadors revolted and assassinated the Spanish viceroy. Full Spanish authority was not restored until 1569.

Peru provided vast amounts of silver and gold for the Spanish treasury. Indigenous peoples and Spaniards born in Peru remained very poor.

Lima's power and influence began to decline during the eighteenth century. The South American colonies gradually split into separate regions such as New Granada and Argentina. Túpac Amaru led a revolt of 60,000 indigenous peoples in 1780. The rebels were defeated within a year. A similar revolted occurred in 1814.

The indigenous people of Peru were rebelling against Spanish rule, but they weren't necessarily concerned with gaining independence. That fell to an outsider. Argentinian General José San Martín had defeated Spanish forces in Chile. His army landed at the port of Pisco in 1820. They proceeded on to Lima the following year. Peru's independence was declared on July 28, 1821.

Spanish forces resisted for three years. Simón Bolívar rallied a large army to finally defeat them in 1824. No strong leader emerged for the new country. A series of Bolivar's officers attempted to maintain order. Bolivian leader Andrés Santa Cruz exploited this turmoil to create a confederation of Peru and Bolivia in 1836. Chilean intervention ended the arrangement three years later.

Stability came in 1844 with General Ramón Castilla's rise to power. Economic growth followed, driven by demand for guano deposits for the European fertilizer market. Slavery was abolished. Railroads and telegraph facilities were built. A liberal constitution was adopted in 1860.

Peru's economy suffered from too much rapid improvement. Spain exploited its economic downturn by attempting to recover the former colony.

A sure-footed llama high in the mountains of Peru.

Peru again defeated the Spanish forces in 1866, with the help of neighboring countries. A defense alliance with Bolivia provoked war with Chile between 1879 and 1883, further debilitating the economy. A succession of dictators ruled the country for the next 25 years.

Peru negotiated a deal with British businessmen in the 1880s, giving them control of the guano mines and railways for sixty-six years. The economy recovered gradually, aided by investments from United States corporations.

President Augusto Leguía began numerous economic reforms in 1908. He traveled to Britain to learn banking and finances, then sought to apply his knowledge to Peru. He had

lands allocated for indigenous people. Leguía failed to carry through with most of his ideas. Protests laid the foundations for the American Revolutionary Popular Alliance (APRA) movement.

Leguía was overthrown in a military coup led by Colonel Luis Sánchez Cerro in 1930. When Sánchez Cerro claimed victory in the 1931 presidential election, APRA staged a revolt in the north. A new constitution was adopted in 1933. Sánchez Cerro was assassinated shortly thereafter. General Oscar Benavides took over as a harsh dictator. He remained in office for six years.

Ceremonial guards drilling in front of the Government Palace in Lima.

Peru

Revolutionary movements declined somewhat as Benavides and his successors promoted considerable economic growth. This situation ended in 1948 when General Manuel Odría exploited political turmoil to stage a *coup d'état*. Odría developed stronger economic and cultural ties with neighboring countries during his presidency.

Manual Prado y Ugarteche became president in 1956. He initiated sweeping economic reforms. The country's finances improved a good deal. Foreign capital flowed into the country as loans and investments. The government won approval for the gradual nationalization of most of the country's oil-production facilities.

General Juan Velasco Alvarado staged a coup in 1968, suspending the constitution to make himself dictator. He gained immediate popularity by nationalizing American-owned businesses. This move created huge tension with the United States. Peru's economy did not improve.

A Peruvian gunboat accosted two U.S. fishing boats off the Peruvian coast in 1969. Peru claimed the boats were trespassing. Tensions with the U.S. increased. The country was devastated by an earthquake in 1970 which killed 66,000 and left some 600,000 homeless. The United States immediately sent relief supplies to aid the victims, despite the events of prior years.

Yet another coup installed General Francisco Morales Bermúdez as president from 1975 to 1980. He instituted austerity measures to reduce debt and inflation. Civilian government returned in 1980, but the failure of the economy to revive gave rise to guerrilla groups called the Shining Path and the Tupac Amaru Revolutionary Movement (MRTA). Substantial government funds were expended in combating their activities.

Alberto Fujimori, a Peruvian of Japanese descent, won the presidency in 1990. He suspended the constitution in 1992 in order to take an iron hand against protest movements.

Several key Shining Path's members were captured. Radical fiscal changes helped stabilize the economy. Fujimori won a second term in 1995.

MRTA guerrillas invaded a reception at the Japanese embassy in 1996, taking 600 hostages. Peruvian forces stormed the building after lengthy negotiations failed. One hostage, two soldiers, and all 14 guerillas were killed. Floods and mudslides in 1998 killed 300 and forced thousands from their homes.

Fujimori was reelected in 2000. He was forced to resign later that year after corruption rumors were verified. Alejandro Toledo Manrique, a respected economist, became Peru's first elected president of indigenous descent in 2001.

The Plaza de Armas at Cuzco.

Philippines

REPUBLIC OF THE PHILIPPINES

Located in Southeast Asia off the coast of Vietnam, the Philippines is comprised of more than 7,000 islands. It is part of the Malay Archipelago. About 1,000 of the islands are inhabited. Most of the islands were formed by volcanoes, so massive mountains are common. Volcanoes become active from time to time and earthquakes are common. The larger islands, particularly Luzon and Mindanao, have broad plains and level, fertile valleys. Lowland areas of the islands are hot and humid most of the year. Destructive typhoons blow in from the surrounding oceans each year.

The majority of Filipinos are of Malay backgrounds. There are also people of Chinese descent and various indigenous groups. The Philippines is predominantly Christian with a small Muslim population. Pilipino and English are the official languages, but many indigenous languages are also spoken.

Fertile volcanic soils and high rainfall make agriculture a key part of the economy. Rice, sugar cane, corn and coconuts are the major crops. Intensive farming of pigs, poultry, goats and water buffalo also occurs. The seas around the islands provide a rich variety of seafoods.

Fine-quality commercial timber is harvested and shipped to world markets.

Nickel, zinc, copper, cobalt, gold, silver and iron ore are extracted in large quantities. The Benguiat gold mines have been a source of wealth for decades. Substantial reserves of oil were discovered in the seas around Palawan in recent years.

Most industry is concentrated in and around Manila. Textiles, processed foods and tobacco products make up the largest percentage of the country's manufacturing output. The importance of durable goods such as furniture, electronic equipment and motor vehicles has grown in recent years.

The memorial to J. P. Rizal, who died in the cause of independence from Spain.

SCOTT BRODIE

Philippines

FLAT EARTH PICTURE GALLERY

Makati, the financial center of the Philippines.

The Philippines has been one of the most democratic nations in Asia, except for a 1972-1981 period of martial law. It has an American-style government with a Congress comprising the House of Representatives (lower house) and a Senate (upper house). Representatives are elected for three years, senators for six years. Presidents are popularly elected for six-year terms and cannot be reelected. The president is assisted by the vice-president, who can hold office for only two successive terms.

Peoples called Negritos migrated to the Philippine islands as early as 25,000 years ago. Most Filipinos are descendents of immigrants from the Asian mainland and Indonesia. A distinct Filipino people had emerged from the mixture of cultures by the fifth century A.D. The Filipinos became active in trade, mining, ship-building and weaving. Islam was introduced in the southern islands by Arab traders.

Spanish explorer, Ferdinand Magellan, arrived in the Philippines on March 17, 1521. Chief Lapu Lapu's forces killed Magellan on Mactan Island, when he tried to impose Spanish authority.

Miguel López de Legazpi founded a Spanish settlement at Cebu in 1564. He named the islands Islas Filipinas after the infant Philip, heir to the Spanish throne.

Settlers landed at Manila five years later. The status of local chiefs was guaranteed if they pledged loyalty to Spain.

Augustinian friars, introduced by Legazpi, began converting the locals to Christianity. Through them, Spanish culture permeated to most parts of the islands. Local priests cooperated with government officials, sending back regular reports to Manila.

Other European nations wanted to develop a presence in the Philippines. The British and the Dutch often launched attacks against Spanish traders through the end of the sixteenth century.

Manila had developed trading links with China, India and the Indonesian archipelago by 1601. The main trade, however, was with Mexico. High-quality silks were carried on government-owned ships called the Manila Galleons. They returned with silver bullion as payment.

Mestizos, people of mixed Spanish–Filipino heritage, acquired large areas of land in the eighteenth century. They established sugar plantations on Negros and leased Catholic lands for rice cultivation. They soon became the elite of the colony.

José P. Rizal began a campaign against Spanish colonialism in the 1880s. The Spanish had him executed. This aroused Filipino spirit even more. Emilio Aguinaldo staged an uprising on Luzon in December

ELECTRA COLLECTION

General Douglas MacArthur (left) wades ashore at Leyte in 1944.

Americans branded them as insurrectionists, sparking a guerrilla war. Thousands were killed in the fighting. Aguinaldo was captured in 1901, swearing allegiance to the U.S. authority.

Military rule was replaced by the civil government in 1902. Governor William H Taft established a bicameral legislature. American teachers spread across the archipelago to pass their expertise on to local teachers.

The Jones Act of 1916 promised independence to the Philippines, but no date was set. The Tydings-McDuffe Bill, passed in 1934, granted absoluate and complete independence to the islands by 1946.

of 1896, surprising the ill-prepared Spanish garrison. A pact was signed in the fall of 1897, in which the Spanish guaranteed certain reforms.

A United States Navy squadron destroyed a Spanish fleet in Manila Bay in May of 1898, during the Spanish-American War. American troops entered Manila in August. Spain ceded the entire archipelago to the U.S. under the terms of the 1898 Treaty of Paris. The U.S. paid Spain $20 million and prepared to use its military to rule the islands.

Aguinaldo had already declared the Philippines independent and established a provisional government. The

It provided for an interim commonwealth supervised by the U.S. with a constitution and the Philippine president elected by the people. Manuel Luis Quezon was elected president.

Japanese troops landed on Luzon and advanced on Manila in 1941. A large-scale invasion soon followed. The occupation and warfare caused widespread damage to the islands. General Douglas MacArthur led a massive Allied landing at Leyte on October 20,1944 against determined Japanese opposition. In Manila, the allies fought them street by street and house by house. More than 400,000 Japanese died. The ground and aerial assault left Manila one of the most ravaged cities of World War II. More than a million Filipinos died.

Manuel Roxas became president in 1946. Full independence followed on July 4, 1946. The United States was granted 99-year leases on its Philippine military bases.

Communist-led Huk guerrillas had become strong while fighting against the Japanese. Now they fought for equitable land redistribution within the independent country. They were neutralized by a massive show of military force and a program of resettlement and land reform. This was instituted in 1953 by President Ramón Magsaysay, but cur-

Some of the thousands of graves in the American World War II cemetery in Manila.

SCOTT BRODIE

tailed after his death in an air crash four years later.

The Philippines was well ahead of its Asian neighbors economically during the 1950s, There were widespread problems with corruption and crime. Ferdinand Marcos, elected president in 1965, faced some huge challenges. The Huks assassinated officials and politicians in Luzon. The Moro National Liberation Front (MNLF), on predominantly Muslim Mindanao Island, violently opposed the resettlement of Christians there.

In 1969, Marcos became the first president elected for a second term. Violence was on the rise. An assassination attempt on Pope Paul VI in 1970 drew international attention. Using the disturbances as an excuse, Marcos imposed martial law in September 1972, claiming this move was necessary for curbing the violence. A new constituion was adopted in 1973. It contained temporary provisions giving Marcos absolute power. Elections were postponed.

Many major industries came under the control of Marcos' friends during this period. Most needed huge government subsidies. The oil crisis of the mid-1970s caused interest rates to skyrocket. Prices for agricultural products fell dramatically.

Marcos lifted martial law in 1981. He won a new six-year presidential term. His long-

time critic Benigno Aquino was murdered at Manila Airport in 1983. A military conspiracy was blamed, but the defendants were acquitted.

Foreign investors withdrew their capital and the economy crumbled. The International Monetary Fund (IMF) agreed to help only if drastic control measures were taken. Inflation soared past sixty percent in 1984. Support for the economy at this time came from the balikbayans, Filipinos working in other countries. Their earnings accounted for fourteen percent of export earnings.

Marcos was defeated by Corazon 'Cory' Aquino, widow of his assassinated opponent in the 1986 elections. Refusing to leave office, Marcos declared himself the winner. Politicians and members of the military defected to Aquino. He was forced to flee the country, allegedly taking with him large amounts of illegally gained wealth. Marcos went into exile in Hawaii, where he died in 1989.

Aquino had little experience in government. The economy was not recovering quickly enough and the military was uneasy. Army rebels staged several coups, all put down by forces loyal to the president. Four provinces on Mindanao were given autonomy as a special Muslim region. The MNLF continued its fight for independ-

ence. U.S. Air Force jets assisted the Philippine government in suppressing a coup attempt in 1989. The Philippine senate voted against continued U.S. presence at its military bases.

Fidel Valdez Ramos, elected in 1992, was the most successful of recent presidents. He revived the economy, encouraged foreign investment and delivered much-needed stability. The MNLF and the Philippine government reached an agreement in 1996, in which nine more provinces were added to the Muslim area on Mindanao. Agitation in other provinces and on other islands was begun by the Moro Islamic Liberation Front (MILF), an offshoot of the MNLF.

Former film star Joseph 'Erap' Estrada was elected president in 1998. By late 2000, it was alleged he had accepted huge financial pay-offs from illegal gambling operators. After disputed impeachment procedures, the Supreme Court removed him from office.

Vice-President Gloria Arroyo took office in 2001. Stability has returned, but major economic challenges remain. Muslim rebels gained special U.S. attention after the September 2001 terrorist attacks on the United States. United States troops are assisting the Philippine forces in dealing with them.

Poland

REPUBLIC OF POLAND

Bordered on the north by the Baltic Sea, Poland is located in central Europe. There are numerous lakes and swamps along the Baltic coast. The balance of the vast northern region is made up of plains and low hills. A series of large, shallow valleys dominate the central areas. The Carpathian and Sudetes mountains lie in the south, on the Czech and Slovak borders. The rest of the landscape, part of the North European Plain, is mostly low lying. The climate is continental, featuring very cold winters and hot summers. Most rainfall occurs during summer months.

Polish society is homogeneous, except for about three percent of the population. There are small minorities of Belorussians and Germans. Most people are Christian. The official language is Polish, although a number of minority languages and dialects are also spoken.

Poland was heavily industrialized during the communist era. Iron and steel are manufactured and there is ship building and repairing on the Baltic coast. Chemicals, textiles and processed foods are other major manufactures. Sulphur, coal, copper, zinc and lead are all mined in large quantities. The large coal mining industry remains in a uncompetitive communist-era structure. Poland ranks as one of the Europe's leading agricultural countries. Potatoes, rye, barley, beet sugar and wheat are primary crops. There is also a substantial dairy industry. Despite the substantial amount of land farmed, the country must rely on imports from other nations to meets its food needs.

A new constitution was adopted in 1997. The president, as head of state, is elected by the people for a five-year term and may be reelected only once. From the members of the parliament, the president selects a prime minister who then selects a cabinet. The parliament is a bicameral body with members of both houses

A young girl selling flowers in Warsaw.

FLAT EARTH PICTURE GALLERY

Poland

The entrance to the Auschwitz extermination camp, which is preserved as a memorial to those who died under the Nazi regime.

being elected for four-year terms.

Slavic tribes migrated to the region of present-day Poland as early as 1500 B.C. These tribes are believed to have united under a king known as Piast about A.D. 840. Mieszko, a descendant of Piast, ruled from 962 to 992. He led the Poles into Christianity, most likely to appease German crusaders. Mieszko's son, Boleslav I, conducted successful wars against Holy Roman Emperor Henry II and considerably expanded his domain. He was crowned king by the pope in 1025. Boleslav's kingdom soon reached beyond the Carpathian Mountains and the Oder and Dnetri rivers.

The empire broke up as dynasty members fell out with each other, beginning in the mid-twelfth century. The Teutonic Knights took this opportunity to establish a base in the northern regions. German colonists also made claims to pieces of land.

King Wladyslaw I was crowned king of the Piast dynasty in 1320. He began reconstructing the empire. Poland flourished under Wladyslaw. This prosperity contined under the reign of his son Casimir III. He initiated many government reforms and founded a university at Krakow. He extended aid to Jewish refugees from western Europe.

Casimir's grand niece, Queen Jadwiga, married Grand Prince Jagiello of neighboring Lithuania in 1386. She died thirteen years later, but Jagiello continued as head of the combined Poland and Lithuania.

The union created one of the most powerful European kingdoms of the time. Its armies broke the power of the Teutonic Knights in 1410. The Jagiello dynasty's lands stretched to the Black Sea. The merger was formalized in 1569 with the Union of Lublin. This was a golden era for Polish influence and culture. Scientific accomplishment was represented by the great astronomer Copernicus.

Poland's elite classes forced the monarch to accept parliamentary government. They maintained the concept of a royal republic under which the monarch was elected from within their ranks. The monarchy was weakened by plots among powerful nobles after King Sigismund II died in 1572

Sweden invaded from the west and Russia invaded from the east in 1655. These invasions met a valiant Polish defense, which limited the loss of territory and maintained a Polish identity. Polish territories such as East Ukraine and North Livonia were lost.

Traditionally dressed musicians in Krakow.

The Russian Empire began a systematic effort to control the weakening Poland in the early eighteen century. Widespread corruption within the Polish nobility accelerated Russian success. Frederick Augustus of Saxony was placed on the throne in 1733. This led to the War of the Polish Succession. By its end, Poland had fallen under Russian control. Russia, Prussia and Austria divided the Polish kingdom among themselves from 1772 to 1795.

The Kingdom of Poland was made an autonomous part of the Russian Empire in 1815. Nationalism led to a revolt in 1830. Polish forces enjoyed initial success but were ultimately defeated. Autonomy was suspended and Poland integrated with Russia. Several more revolts culminated in the January Revolution of 1863.

Russia then began the complete integration of Poland into Russian society. The Russian language was introduced in schools, while Polish was restricted. Culture, politics, and economics were transformed in an effort to make much of Poland into provinces of Russia.

Polish nationalist armies aligned themselves with Germany and Austria in World War I. They saw this as a way of breaking free of Russian control.

Poland became independent on November 9, 1918. The Treaty of Versailles failed to restore Poland's 1772 border with Russia. The two countries went to war. The Poles inflicted a severe defeat on the Red Army, taking parts of the Ukraine, Lithuania and Belorussia. The Treaty of Riga in 1921 confirmed the new boundaries.

Disturbed by a succession of shaky coalition governments, Joseph Pilsudski staged a *coup d'état* in May 1926. Ignacy Moscicki was installed as president. Pilsudski, as minister of war, gradually acquired control of the country up until his death in 1935.

Poland was a central player in events leading up to World War II. Nazi Germany demanded Poland surrender the port of Gdansk on the Baltic coast. The Soviet Union and Germany signed a non-aggression pact in August. It included details of how Poland would be partitioned between them.

Germany invaded Poland on September 1, 1939. Britain and France gave Germany an ultimatum to withdraw. When it failed to do so, those nations declared war on September 3rd. The Soviet Union invaded Poland from the east.

Germany began a barbaric regime in western Poland. Millions were killed, including about three million Jews sent to concentration camps. A Polish government in exile was established in London. Polish forces that had escaped the invasion

A memorial to fighters who resisted the Nazis in World War II.

Poland

fought alongside the Allies. Thousands of Poles joined resistance movements in an effort to thwart the German intruders. Germany invaded the Soviet Union during the early 1940s. It then controlled all of Poland.

The Soviet Union joined the Allies in August of 1944. Its forces penetrated Poland, establishing a provisional Polish government at Lublin. Resistance members organized a revolt against the Germans in Warsaw. The Soviet army declined to give support. The revolt was crushed by the Germans.

The Soviets finally entered Warsaw in January of 1945. Six months later a new government dominated by the pro-communist Polish Workers' Party was created. The Soviet Union acquired a large part of eastern Poland.

The communists gained firm control of Poland in the elections of 1947. Those elections were denounced by the U.S. as fraudulent. The communists immediately dissolved all opposition parties. Industry was fully nationalized and some collectivization of agriculture began within a few years. Unlike other communist states, Poland retained privately owned farms throughout the communist years.

A new constitution in 1952 made Poland a people's republic, along Soviet lines. Christianity was banned and its followers persecuted. Discontent with Soviet control simmered in the 1950s. Widespread demonstrations in 1956 led to a more liberal government led by Wladyslaw Gomulka.

Industrial problems simmered in the shipyards and coal mines. Strikes in October 1980 forced the government to allow the formation of trade unions and the right to strike. Most prominent of the new unions was Solidarity, led by electrician Lech Walesa.

Millions flocked to support Solidarity, throwing the government into chaos. After several other national leaders failed, General Wojciech Jaruzelsji was made party chief and prime minister. Solidarity's demands for free elections alarmed the government to such an extent it declared martial law. Unions were banned and Walesa and his colleagues were arrested and imprisoned.

Various non-communist nations imposed sanctions, which deepened Poland's dire economic state. Walesa was released after eleven months and martial law was ended in 1983.

Solidarity continued to attract widespread support. It participated in negotiations that led to free elections in 1989. Solidarity won a huge majority and Walesa was elected president that year.

Economic reform brought change very slowly. Continued hardship made it difficult for people to remain patient. A succession of governments and prime ministers followed through the 1990s. Constitutional revisions of 1997 reduced the powers of the president.

Poland joined the North Atlantic Treaty Organization (NATO) in 1999. Its membership in the European Union (EU) is expected to be approved in 2003.

The Palace of Culture, a stark remnant of Poland's communist era.

FLAT EARTH PICTURE GALLERY

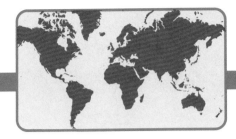

Portugal

PORTUGUESE REPUBLIC

GOVERNMENT
Website www.portugal.gov.pt
Capital Lisbon
Type of government Republic
Voting Universal adult suffrage
Head of state President
Head of government Prime
Minister
Constitution 1976
Legislature
Unicameral Assembly of the
Republic
Judiciary Supreme Court
Member of CE, EU, IMF, NATO,
OECD, UN, UNESCO, WHO, WTO

LAND AND PEOPLE
Land area 35,446 sq mi (91,831 sq
km)
Highest point Ponta do Pico
7,713 ft (2,351 m)
Coastline
1,114 mi (1,793 km)
Population 10,066,253
Major cities and populations
Lisbon 3,826,000
Porto 1,922,000
Ethnic groups
Portuguese 99%, African 1%
Religion Christianity
Languages Portuguese (official)

ECONOMIC
Currency Euro
Industry
textiles, footwear; wood pulp, paper,
cork products, oil refining,
chemicals, fisheries, wine, tourism
Agriculture
grain, potatoes, olives, grapes,
sheep, cattle, goats, poultry, beef,
dairy
Natural resources
seafood, cork, tungsten, iron ore,
uranium ore, marble

Portugal is located on the Atlantic coast of the Iberian Peninsula in southwestern Europe. The country also includes the Azores and the Madeira island groups in the Atlantic Ocean. The Rio Tejo flows through the center of the country. The mountainous landscape in the north is part of the Galacian Mountains which extend from Spain. The coastline features a wide fertile plain which rises inland.

Climatic conditions vary between north and south. The south, particularly along the coast, has a warm Mediterranean climate. The north is heavily affected by the Atlantic Ocean, so it is cooler. In the eastern regions, and at the higher altitudes, temperatures are lower. Very little rain falls in the summer months.

Most people are native Portugese. There is a small minority of African-descended peoples who migrated from Portugal's former colonies. Christianity is the dominant religion. Portuguese is the official language.

About 32 percent of Portugal's land is forested. The country is one of the largest producers of cork in the world. It also mills a large quantity of roundwood.

Commercial fishing is important to the economy. Large fishing fleets operate along the coast. Sardines and tuna make up much of the catch.

Agriculture is not as sophisticated as in many other European countries. Potatoes, grapes, tomatoes, corn, wheat and olives are primary crops. Portugal is one of the world's leading producers of olive oil and wine.

Manufacturing continues to grow. Principal products now include processed foods, textiles, machinery, motor vehicles, chemicals and refined petroleum. Products of smaller industries, including lace, pottery and tiles, are world famous.

Tourism is a major industry for Portugal. Regions in the south, such as the Algarve, attract huge numbers of visitors from other parts of Europe.

A new constitution was enacted in 1976 following the overthrow of the previous dictatorship. It was amended in 1982, 1989, 1992 and 1997. The president is elected for a five-year term by a vote of the people. The president appoints the prime minister, who in turn appoints a cabinet from members of the unicameral legislature. Members of the legislature are elected for four years by popular vote based on proportional representation.

Portugal was first settled around 1000 B.C. by Celtic tribes collectively known as the Lusitanians. Phoenicians established

Portugal

trading posts along the coast in the third century B.C. The Roman Empire invaded Portugal in the second century B.C. Conquest was varied as some tribes resisted more vigorously than others. Rome gradually became dominant and the area adopted its culture. Christianity was adopted. The Portuguese language evolved from the Latin introduced by the Romans.

Germanic Visigoths swept across the land in the early fifth century A.D. They conquered all but the Suevi kingdom in the north. The Algarve region became a part of the Byzantine Empire during the sixth and seventh centuries.

The Moors crossed from northern Africa to conquer almost all the Iberian Peninsula in about 712. Their culture, particularly its scientific aspects, had a profound effect. The Moors tolerated Christianity, but conversion to Islam was widespread.

Viking raids on the coast weakened Moorish authority at the end of the eighth century. This began a long, arduous campaign to expel the Moors. Ferdinand I of Castile had conquered much of the country by 1064.

Henry of Burgundy became the first Count of Portugal in 1095. His son, Alfonso I, after winning a decisive victory against the Moors, became king in 1143.

The eccentric architecture of Pena Castle at Sintra.

The Pope acknowledged the Portuguese monarchy in 1179. The Moors were finally expelled from Portugal by King Alfonso III in 1249.

As regions were taken from the Moors, many former serfs were freed and given land. Charters of rights were drawn up for the various municipalities. Portugal was regularly at war with Castile during much of this time. When King Ferdinand I died in 1383, Castile tried to usurp the Portuguese crown. Portugal defeated Castile at the Battle of Aljubarrota two years later. John I became king of the Aviz dynasty. Portugal and Britain became permanent allies with

A fisher working on nets in Olhao's harbor.

the signing of the Treaty of Windsor the following year.

When the withdrawing Moors were pursued into northern Africa, the Portuguese gained a taste for colonial expansion. They became the first major European explorers and colonizers. Their ships explored the African coast.

Portugese navigators claimed the Azores and Madeiras early in the fifteenth century. Ceuta, in Morroco, was captured in 1415. Bartholomew Dias became the first European to round the Cape of Good Hope in 1488.

The 1494 Treaty of Tordesillas divided the uncharted lands of the New World between Portugal and Spain. Neither country had much idea what they were getting. Vasco da Gama made two important voyages of discovery in 1498 and 1502. Pedro Alvarez Cabral discovered and claimed Brazil in 1500. Various parts of Asia such as Malacca, Goa and Hormuz were taken as trading posts.

The Aviz dynasty died out in 1580. King Philip II of Spain seized Portugal. Britain and the Netherlands annexed many former Portuguese colonial territories during wars that followed.

Spain became absorbed in another war in 1640. The Portuguese reestablished their sover-

eignty. King John IV became monarch. Spain recognized independent Portugal in 1668. Portugal reclaimed Brazil from the Dutch. Gold and diamonds from Brazil helped stabilize the economy by the middle of the eighteenth century.

The alliance with Britain brought conflict to Portugal in 1807. France, while at war with Britain, invaded Portugal. The royal family fled to Brazil. British forces, led by Arthur Wellesley, later the Duke of Wellington, landed in Portugal in 1809. The ensuing Peninsular War saw British and Portuguese forces eventually drive the French out in 1811.

King John VI returned from Brazil to take the throne of Portugal in 1816. Four years later he accepted a new, liberal constitution which established a monarchy. Brazil gained its independence in 1822 with John's son, Pedro I, as emperor.

Pedro succeeded to the throne of Portugal in 1826. He abdicated in favor of his daughter Maria II. Another of John VI's sons, Dom Miguel, seized the throne in 1826. Pedro ousted him, with the help of Spain, Britain and France. Maria was restored to the throne in 1834 and reigned until 1853. Considerable social, legal and commercial reforms were enacted during this time.

Allegations of corruption provoked King Carlos I to dis-

Portugal

FLAT EARTH PICTURE GALLERY

A cable tram on a steep incline in Lisbon.

ernment. He was elected president two years later. Carmana's finance minister, António de Oliveira Salazar, was largely responsible for stabilizing the national economy. Salazar became prime minister and dictator in 1932.

Salazar introduced a new constitution giving himself even more power the next year. Although neutral in World War II, Portugal did permit the Allies to use the Azores for air bases. Post-war changes to electoral rules altered very little in the government. Salazar's secret police effectively crushed any challenge to his position.

Portugal fell steadily behind the pace of progress in the rest of Europe during the 1950s and 1960s. It became embroiled in independence wars with its African colonies of Angola, Mozambique and Portuguese Guinea. The press was censored and any protest movements were ruthlessly suppressed during the 1960s.

Salazar suffered a stroke in 1968 and was replaced by Marcello Caetano. There was some relaxing of the strict state controls, but not enough to satisfy the mood for change. A group of Portugese army officers, led by General António de Spinola, deposed the government on

April 25, 1974. The coup became known as the Captains' Revolution.

Spinola, who had promised democracy for the country, resigned after only five months as president. Communists attempted to gain power, but were narrowly defeated. A provisional military group took control. Banks and other industries were nationalized and large scale land reform began.

São Tomé and Principe, Cape Verde, Angola, Portuguese Guinea and Mozambique all achieved independence in 1975. East Timor declared its independence in 1975 as well, but was later invaded by Indonesia. Goa had been seized by India in 1961. This left Macau, on the edge of China, as the sole remaining colony. The return of troops and settlers to Portugal from the newly independent nations increased unemployment and unrest.

A new constitution was adopted in 1976. Portugal returned to civilian rule. The economy remained sluggish during the 1980s and 1990s, as a number of short-term administrations made attempts at recovery.

Portugal campaigned against brutal Indonesian control of its former colony, East Timor. This led to a vote for independence organized by the United Nations. Macau was returned to Chinese control in 1999.

miss parliament. He created a dictatorship under João Franco in 1906. Charles and his heir were assassinated two years later. His successor, Manuel II, ruled for two years before being forced to abdicate by a republican revolution.

Constant conflicts with the Catholic church arose in subsequent years as the government sought to limit the church's power. Disillusioned republicans staged numerous coups and uprisings from 1917 onwards. Economic conditions deteriorated rapidly.

A coup of 1926 deposed the fortieth government since the republic was proclaimed. General António Carmana was selected to head the new gov-

Puerto Rico

COMMONWEALTH OF PUERTO RICO

Puerto Rico is located in the Caribbean Sea as one of the larger islands of the West Indies. The nation includes smaller islands such as Culebra, Mona and Vieques. The main island's mountainous terrain is dominated by the Cordillera Central. There is a fertile coastal plain on the northern side. The climate is tropical with consistent warm temperatures and rainfall throughout the year.

Most Puerto Ricans have Spanish ancestors. Some have a mixed Spanish and indigenous-background while others are descendants of African slaves. Puerto Rico is predominantly Catholic. Spanish and English are the official languages.

Arawak immigrants in the ninth century A.D. named the island Boriquén. Christopher Columbus renamed it San Juan Bautista in 1493. Spaniard Juan Ponce de León landed at the harbor he called Puerto Rico, or rich port, in 1508. The resistance of the indigenous people was met with force. Many of them died from diseases carried by the Europeans. African slaves worked the sugar plantations from 1513. Attacks by British and Dutch groups led to the fortification of San Juan in the early eighteenth century. Independence movements, including the 1868 Lares Rebellion, were suppressed by the Spanish.

United States forces landed on Puerto Rico during the Spanish–American War of 1898. A bicameral congress was established and Washington appointed a governor to administer the island in 1900. The Jones Act of 1917 made Puerto Rico a U.S. territory and its people American citizens.

American investment flowed in. With free access to American markets, sugar cane became the predominant industry. Although the economy declined rapidly in the 1930s, the island benefited from President Franklin Roosevelt's New Deal program.

Governors were popularly elected, beginning in 1948. Governor Muñoz Marín launched a campaign to lessen the economic reliance on sugar. Taxation concessions drew electronics, pharmaceutical and clothing corporations to the island.

The people chose to remain a self-governing commonwealth in association with the United States in 1967. The North American Free Trade Agreement (NAFTA) led to the loss of low-wage jobs to Mexico. Sila María Calderón won the 2000 elections, making her the nation's first female governor. Residents and environmentalists have long protested the use of Vieques Island for U.S. military munitions testing. The U. S. government has agreed to terminate those tests by 2003.

Qatar

STATE OF QATAR

Comprising the mainland and several offshore islands, Qatar is located on a peninsula on the western side of the Persian Gulf. The peninsula is flat, rising no more than about 325 feet (100 m) at the Dukhan Heights in the west. Almost all of the landscape is arid, rocky desert and salt flats. Rainfall is minimal and temperatures are hot through most of the year. Humidity is very high at all times.

Almost all of Qatar's population lives in the capital, Doha, or other urban areas. Arabs make up the largest ethnic group, accounting for forty percent of the people. Pakistanis, Indians, Iranians and native-born Qataris makes up most of the balance. Nearly all of the population is Sunni Muslim, of the Wahhabi sect. Arabic is the official language.

Petroleum and natural gas account for about eighty percent of the country's export income. Some fruits and vegetables are grown. Most agriculture is devoted to livestock.

Despite its inhospitable nature, Qatar peninsula has been inhabited since the Stone Age. The first known inhabitants were the Canaanites. It was controlled by the Ottoman Empire until the late eighteen century when it passed to the Wahhabi sect of Islam. In the mid-eighteenth century the Bani Utib people from Kuwait established a fishing industry at Subarah.

Turkish control was established in 1871 through the ruling Thani dynasty. Qatar became a British protectorate in 1916, but it was still ruled as an absolute monarchy under the Thanis. The main industries were fishing and pearling until 1949, when oil was discovered.

Independence from Britain came in 1971. The new constitution provided for an assembly elected by the people and a council of advisers appointed by the sheikh. Sheikh Ahmad ibn Ali al-Thani was overthrown in a 1972 palace coup. His cousin, Khalifa ibn Hamad al-Thani, took over as ruler. The family nationalized the oil industry and launched a large industrialization and development program.

Qatar was used as a base by Allied forces during the Gulf War in 1991. The nation has a defense agreement with the United States.

Hamad bin Khalifa al-Thani, architect of much of the development, deposed his father in June 1995. Controls on the media were loosened and relations with Iraq, Iran and Israel improved. Women were given the right to vote in the 1999 elections. Qatar settled territorial disputes with Bahrain and Saudi Arabia in 2001.

GOVERNMENT
Website english.mofa.gov.qa
Capital Doha
Type of government Traditional monarchy
Independence from Britain September 3, 1971
Voting none
Head of state Emir
Head of government Prime Minister
Constitution 1972
Legislature Appointed unicameral Advisory Council
Judiciary Court of Appeal
Member of AL, IMF, OPEC, UN, UNESCO, WHO, WTO

LAND AND PEOPLE
Land area 4,416 sq mi (11,437 sq km)
Highest point Qurayn Abu al Bawl 338 ft (103 m)
Coastline 350 mi (563 km)
Population 769,152
Major cities and populations Doha 391,000 Ar-Rayyan 161,000
Ethnic groups Arab 40%, Pakistani 18%, Indian 18%, Iranian 10%, others 14%
Religions Islam 95%, others 5%
Languages Arabic (official)

ECONOMIC
Currency riyal
Industry oil refining, fertilizers, petrochemicals
Agriculture fruits, vegetables, poultry, dairy, beef
Natural resources petroleum, natural gas, seafood

Romania

GOVERNMENT
Website www.guv.ro
Capital Bucharest
Type of government Republic
Independence from Ottoman Empire May 8, 1877
Voting Universal adult suffrage
Head of state President
Head of government Prime Minister
Constitution 1991
Legislature
Bicameral Parliament
Chamber of Deputies (lower house),
Senate (upper house)
Judiciary Supreme Court
Member of CE, IMF, NATO, UN, UNESCO, WHO, WTO

LAND AND PEOPLE
Land area 91,700 sq mi
(237,500 sq km)
Highest point Moldoveanu
8,343 ft (2,543 m)
Coastline 140 mi (225 km)
Population 22,364,022
Major cities and populations
Bucharest 2,400,000
Iasi 350,000
Timisoara 340,000
Ethnic groups Romanian 90%,
Hungarian 9%, others 1%
Religions Christianity
Languages Romanian (official)

ECONOMIC
Currency Leu
Industry
textiles, footwear, machinery, motor
vehicles, mining, timber,
construction materials, metallurgy,
chemicals, food processing,
petroleum refining
Agriculture
wheat, corn, beet sugar, sunflower
seeds, potatoes, grapes, eggs, sheep
Natural resources
petroleum, timber, natural gas,
coal, iron ore, salt

Romania is in southeastern Europe, with a coastline on the Black Sea. The Transylvania Basin, or Plateau, occupies much of central Romania. It is almost completely surrounded by mountain ranges, the largest of which is the Carpathians. The Danube River flows along Romania's borders with Yugoslavia and Bulgaria. Romania's climate is continental with warm to hot summers and cool winters. Cool to cold temperatures prevail in the mountains.

Ninety percent of the people are Romanian. Most of the balance is Hungarian. Nearly all of the people are Christians, most of whom belong to the Romanian Orthodox Church. Romanian is the official language, with four major dialects.

Romania today covers most of the area occupied by ancient Dacia. Roman colonizers arrived in A.D. 106. They remained until 273, giving the country its name and introducing Christianity.

Invasions by Goths, Huns, Avars, Bulgars and Magyars through the ninth century had a profound effect on Romanian culture. Most people converted to Orthodox Christianity.

The people of Bulgaria developed two principalities called Walachia and Moldavia south and east of the Carpathian Mountains. They came under the control of the Ottoman Turks in 1526. Michael the Brave of Walachia united the two principalities in the sixteenth century, hoping to gain independence from the Turks. He was assassinated in 1601 and control reverted back to the Turks.

The princes of Moldavia and Walachia formed a disastrous alliance with Russia in the early eighteenth century. This only led to renewed Turkish control. Most Romanians were reduced to serfdom or a nomadic existence.

Russia went to war against the Turks in 1774. The Turks loosened their control over Moldavia and Walachia. Russia tried to exert power over the area in the following decades, but the spirit of independence

Rollerblading in a Bucharest park.

FLAT EARTH PICTURE GALLERY

Romania

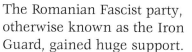

FLAT EARTH PICTURE GALLERY

had grown too strong. Colonel Alexandru Ion Cuza was elected as prince of the two regions, uniting them as the principality of Romania.

Romania's declaration of independence in May of 1877 was recognized by the Treaty of Berlin the following year. Prince Carol of Hohenzollern-Sigmaringen was crowned king in 1881.

Despite King Carol's declaration of his country's neutrality during World War I, Austro-German and Bulgarian armies occupied Romania by 1917. The country had no choice but to take part in the fighting. Treaties at the end of the war granted territories to Romania which doubled its area.

The Liberal party and the National Peasants' party fought for control of the country. Weak economic conditions led to growing political dissension.

The Romanian Fascist party, otherwise known as the Iron Guard, gained huge support.

The Soviet Union occupied Romania at the outset of World War II. Germany, in alliance with the Soviets at that point, also established a presence in Romania.

King Carol II named Ion Antonescu, an Iron Guard sympathizer, as dictator. The king abdicated in favor of his son Michael in 1940. The real power was in the hands of Antonescu. Romania joined Germany's attack on the Soviet Union.

The Soviets returned to Romania in 1944. King Michael deposed Antonescu and surrendered to the Soviets.

The Communist Party established a people's republic in December 1947, forcing King Michael to abdicate. A new constitution, based on that of the

USSR, was adopted in 1948. Nationalization of industry and collectivization of the farming sector began.

The economy of Romania became increasing strong during the 1950s and 1960s. Nicolae Ceausescu, a harsh and authoritarian leader, took over as president in 1965. The Workers' Party became the Romanian Communist Party with Ceausescu as general-secretary.

Romania was heavily in debt to Western nations by the 1980s. Extreme austerity measures intended to counteract this burden made life difficult for most Romanians.

Ceausescu's brutal suppression of antigovernment voices turned the army against him. Ceaucesecu and his wife fled the country in 1989. They were soon captured and executed.

Ion Iliescu, a former Ceausescu associate, won the multiparty elections of 1990. A new constitution was adopted in 1991. Tougher economic reform led to more violent uprisings.

A 1994 referendum determined that Moldova, a former Soviet republic of ethnic Romanians, should not unite with Romania. Iliescu lost the presidency to anti-Communist Emil Constantinescu in 1996. Iliescu was reelected in 2000.

Russia

RUSSIAN FEDERATION

Russia is geographically the largest country on Earth, covering nearly seven million square miles (17 million square kilometers). It stretches from the Baltic Sea in the west, across northern Europe and northern Asia, to the Pacific Ocean in the east. The Arctic Ocean lies to the north. It is divided into European Russia and Siberian Russia by the Ural Mountains. On the west side of the Urals is the relatively low-lying East European Plain. To the east are the Siberian Steppes. Rugged mountain ranges separate Russia from Mongolia and China. Northern Siberia is mostly plains interrupted by thousands of lakes. Much of central Siberia is a high plateau.

Russia has many climatic variations throughout its vast area. Temperatures are subarctic in northern Siberia. The balance of Siberia is cool for much of the year. The west and east areas are more continental with high humidity. The south- central region near the Mongolian border is quite hot and arid. The heaviest regular rains fall west of the Ural Mountains.

More than eighty percent of the population is ethnically Russian, but there are at least sixty other ethnic groups. Russia's population has decreased since the demise of the Soviet Union. The very low birth rate has been only partially countered by immigration from former Soviet regions.

Religions were suppressed during the Soviet era. This is no longer the case, but at least two-thirds of the population still claims no religious affiliation. More than twenty million are Russian Orthodox Christians. Islam has a strong following in some regions and there are about a million Jews.

Russian is the official language, written in the Cyrillic script. The diverse ethnic groups speak over a hundred languages and dialects.

Russia's economy relies heavily on industry. Much of the industry is located on the European side of the Ural Mountains. Factories in the northwest produce electronic

FLAT EARTH PICTURE GALLERY

Russia

The ornate grandeur of St. Basil's Cathedral in Moscow's Red Square.

equipment, instruments, machine tools and chemicals, along with a major ship-building and repair industry. The central European region has similar industries, as well as clothing, textiles, farm machinery and railroad cars. The Urals region is the heart of Russia's iron and steel production. Oil is refined and iron and steel produced in western Siberia.

Principal crops in the central European region are vegetables, wheat, cotton, oilseed and fruits. Further east, in the North Caucasus, there is extensive cultivation of beet sugar and wheat. Western Siberia produces wheat, oats, beet sugar and rice.

Mining is a key economic aspect of Russia's central European region. It has large coal mines, substantial oil, iron ore and bauxite reserves. The North Caucasus is similarly rich in oil, natural gas and coal. Manganese, iron ore and aluminium are mined in the Urals, which also has large oil fields. Eastern Siberia holds rich deposits of gold, iron ore, alumina, lead, zinc and coal. Gold and diamonds are mined in the far eastern regions.

The Russian Federation is a republic under the constitution of December 1993. It comprises twenty-one republics, one autonomous region, ten autonomous national areas, forty-nine Russian regions and six Russian territories. The whole nation is grouped into seven administrative districts: the Northwest, Central, Volga, North Caucasus, Urals, Siberia and Far East districts.

The president, who has substantial powers, is elected by the people. The Federal Assembly is bicameral. Russia's upper house is the Federation Council, which consists of members appointed by the governments of the republics, territories and regions. The lower house is the State Duma, whose members are elected according to a system which combines direct and proportional representation. The prime minister is appointed by the president and approved by the Federal Assembly.

Russia was inhabited as far back as the Palaeolithic era. The northern Eurasian plains were home to nomadic groups around 2000 B.C. Most prominent of these was the Scythians, who reached the zenith of their power in the seventh century B.C. Greeks traded with the Scythians on the shores of the Black Sea. The Samarians displaced the Scythians in the third century B.C.

Much of the vast Russian area was thinly populated until the third century A.D. when various groups began invading.

First came the Goths from the Germanic regions to the west, then the Huns swept in from the east in the fourth century. Avars were infiltrating from the Balkans by the sixth century. Slavic people were migrating to the Carpathian region.

Varangians arrived in the western region at the end of the ninth century. It is believed they coined the term 'Russ'. In 882 the Varangian leader, Oleg, transferred his capital from Novgorod to Kiev, where he established the Kievan Rus. This confederation of trading settlements straddled the caravan routes between Europe and China.

The Kievan Rus, under Vladimir the Great, converted to Orthodox Christianity. Vladimir married Anne, sister of Byzantine emperor Basil III. Byzantine culture became a primary influence in architecture, art and music.

Valdimir died in 1015 and his son Yaroslav eventually became ruler. The Kievan Rus reached its greatest power during this time. Yaroslav made Kiev an imperial capital with grand buildings, including the Hagia Sophia. He built schools and enacted new laws.

After Yaroslav's death in 1054, the empire was broken up as his sons divided the lands.

A flower seller on the streets of St. Petersburg.

Mongolian Tatar armies, led by Batu Khan, destroyed much of the region between 1237 and 1240. It was absorbed into the Tatar Empire stretching from Europe to the Pacific Ocean. Lithuania gained control of Belarus and much of the Ukraine.

The principalities were in rebellion against Tatar control by the late fourteenth century. Armies led by the Russian princes engaged the Tatars in battle at Kulikovo Polye in 1380. The most prominent of these princes was Dmitri Donskoy of Muscovy, who ruled from 1359 to 1389.

Russia

Selling artwork in St. Petersburg.

Muscovy, or Moscow, gained supremacy over the other principalities during the reign of Grand Duke Prince Ivan III from 1462 to 1505. Ivan III acquired much of the territory that would form today's Russia. Having married the niece of the last Byzantine emperor, he believed he was heir to the Byzantine Empire.

A new era began in 1547 with seventeen-year-old Ivan IV's coronation as Czar of all the Russias. Known as Ivan the Terrible, he greatly expanded the Russian domain, expelling the Tatars from Astrakhan and Kazan in the 1550s. His reign, which lasted until 1584, was marked by despotism and cruelty. He crushed the power of the nobles and expanded Russia into western Siberia.

Ivan's successor was his weak son, Fyodor, with whom the dynasty ended in 1598. His brother-in-law, Boris Godunov, was elected czar by a national council. However, the empire was in rapid decline by the time Boris died in 1605.

The years following were ones of turmoil. There was no obvious successor to the throne, so various pretenders seized power. Most prominent of these was Basil Shuysky, a noble with Polish backing. Poland's King Sigismund III invaded Russia in 1609, taking Moscow the following year. Cossack forces, led by Prince Dmitry Pozharski, expelled them three years later.

A national council of nobles, clergy, bureaucrats and businessmen chose Michael Romanov as czar in 1613. He was the first of the Romanov dynasty which would rule Russia for the next three centuries. He began the slow modernization of Russian society.

Michael's successor, Alexis, took the eastern Ukraine from Poland. The nobles initially resisted his centralization of power. He overcame their objections by granting them vast tracts of land and control of the peasants.

Russia had not benefited from the social and commercial advances made by the rest of Europe. Change began under the rule of Peter the Great, from 1696 to 1725. Peter took direct control of the Orthodox church, modernized industry and substantially reformed government administration. He encouraged education. A new capital was built at St Petersburg.

Territorial holdings were expanded south to the Black Sea at the expense of the Turkish Ottoman Empire. For the next two centuries Russia and the Ottomans waged almost constant war with each other. Russia usually triumphed. The fomer Muscovite state became known as the Russian Empire.

Russia had four emperors between 1725 and 1741. During the Seven Years War between Prussia and Austria from 1756, Empress Elizabeth backed Austria. In 1762 Peter III took power, but the same year his wife Catherine deposed him. Following his assassination, she became Empress Catherine II, known as Catherine the Great.

Catherine was a dominant personality who strengthened centralized control and expanded Russia's territory further. She also encouraged science, arts and literature. Russia was a leading European power by the end of her reign in 1796. Under her successors, Russia gained Finland and Bessarabia.

Russia joined Great Britain, Sweden, and Austria against Napoleon of France at the beginning of the nineteenth century. A peace agreement was reached in 1807. Napoleon launched his ill-judged invasion of Russia in 1812. Joined by its allies, Russia pushed the French back into France.

The ideas of democracy and nationalism began permeating Russian society during this time. When Nicholas I died in 1825, a group called the Decembrists staged a coup. Their attempt to prevent Nicholas II from taking the throne failed. Most were executed. Nicholas II worked to suppress liberal thinking in order to discourarge further coup attempts.

An uprising in the Russian-controlled Polish kingdom prompted Nicholas to remove

The grandeur of St. Isaac's Cathedral, St. Petersburg.

the Polish monarch. He also helped Austria put down the Hungarian Revolution of 1849. Russia went to war with the Ottomans over the Crimean region, on the Black Sea, in 1854. With British and French support, the Ottomans defeated Russia.

Emperor Alexander II came to power during the Crimean War. Initially a liberal, he was responsible for the emancipation of the serfs in 1861. These were peasants who were permanently bonded to large landowners. He also reorganized public administration, the legal system and the education system. He expanded Russia's territories into the central Asian region and to the Pacific coast of Asia.

Anarchist groups flourished under Alexander II. The most aggressive of these, a populist movement called the nraodniki, was responsible for his assassination on March 1, 1881.

Alexander III ruled from 1881 to 1894. He instituted strict censorship laws and placed controls on intellectual activities. Oppression of Jews was particularly severe under Alexander II. They were forced to live in specific areas and forbidden to enter certain professions. Many were killed. Increased industrialization meant more workers were hired. Working conditions were often deplorable.

Vladimir Ilych Ulyanov, who called himself Lenin, founded the League of the Struggle for the Emancipation of the Working Class in 1895. Three years later the league merged with other groups which promoted the doctrines of Karl Marx. It became the Russian Social

Russia

A young boy sells chess sets on the streets of Moscow.

Democratic Labor Party. The party split into Bolshevik and Menshevik factions in 1903, following internal disputes.

Russia went to war with Japan in 1904 over territory in Manchuria. This war, which Russia lost, was immensely unpopular with Russians. Thousands of people gathered outside the czar's Winter Palace on January 22, 1905. They demanded improved workers' rights as well as an end to the war. Troops fired on them, killing more than 200 on what became known as Bloody Sunday.

The following year saw widespread demonstrations, both peaceful and violent. Czar Nicholas II was moved to increase civil liberties and establish a parliament, the Duma, which met in 1906. Half-hearted attempts were made to provide land rights for peasants between 1906 and 1911. Growing industrialization had created a many workers with specialized skills. Their demands for improved working conditions were supported by the Social Democrats.

A Serbian revolutionary assassinated Archduke Franz Ferdinand of Austria–Hungary at Sarajevo in June of 1914. As a result, Austria–Hungary declared war on Serbia. Nicholas mobilized Russia's forces against Austria–Hungary. Germany declared war on Russia and France. Germany's invasion of Belgium brought Britain into the war on the side of France and Russia.

The conflict was disastrous for Russia. It was surrounded by Germany, Austria–Hungary and Turkey. Russia's supply lines from Britain and France were long and difficult. Food was in short supply and inflation was rampant by 1917. The Russian army performed poorly against the Germans. The troops and the Russian population at large were extremely disheartened.

Socialists staged mass demonstrations in most Russ-ian cities in March of 1917. Workers went on strike all across the country. Troops were ordered to fire on demonstrators. Instead they joined them. The besieged Nicholas abdicated on March 15, 1917. His brother, Michael, refused to accept the throne. This was the end of the Russian empire.

A provisional government was established, headed by the moderate Prince Lvov. His attempts to control the military failed as tens of thousands of troops mutinied. Lvov banned the Bolsheviks, who were believed to be responsible for ongoing riots. The central government was losing control. The Bolshevik soviets, or councils, were threatening his authority. Lvov resigned in favor of Alexander Kerensky.

Lenin, who had been in exile in Switzerland, returned to Russia in April of 1917. Lenin led a bloodless Bolshevik coup against the provisional government the following November. The Council of People's Commissars was established with Lenin as chairman and Leon Trotsky as foreign minister. Laws were reformed, church

* Russia used the Julian calendar until February 1918, when the Gregorian calendar was adopted in line with western Europe. The Gregorian calendar is thirteen days ahead of the Julian, and so the date of the Bolshevik takeover is often quoted as October 25, 1917.

property seized and banks nationalized. A central planning committee was formed to manage the economy, and workers' committees began running factories.

Russia's army withdrew from the war. Russia was forced to hand over large areas of its territory to Germany and Austria–Hungary, under the Treaty of Brest-Litovsk in March of 1918. Russian-dominated Estonia, Finland, Latvia, Ukraine, Lithuania, Azerbaijan, Armenia and Georgia all declared independence from Russia when the revolution began.

Socialist revolutionaries won a majority of seats in the new Constituent Assembly in 1918. However, they refused to accept domination by the All-Russian Congress of Soviets. Lenin dissolved the assembly, and Russia slipped into civil war.

The Bolshevik control of regions such as the Ukraine was opposed by the White Army. This collection of anti-Bolsheviks led by former army officers was supported by European powers and the United States. Lenin used the turmoil as an excuse to make his newly renamed All-Russian Communist Party the only legal political party.

This statue celebrates the farm collectivization program — created in 1937, it is typical of Soviet-era sculptures.

FLAT EARTH PICTURE GALLERY

Russia

The Winter Palace in St. Petersburg was home to the czar until the 1917 revolution

An intervention force of British, French and United States troops landed at Murmansk in northern Russia in March of 1918. It had little impact and withdrew late the following year. The Bolshevik Red Army pushed the failing White Army eastward, finally defeating it. Thousands of its supporters fled to China.

The Bolsheviks controlled much of Russia by 1920. Bids for independence by Ukraine, Belorussia, Azerbaijan, Georgia and Armenia were crushed. The civil war and war with Poland in 1920–21 had left much of Russia in ruins. Famine in 1920 saw hundreds of thousands die of starvation.

Lenin retreated from full-scale communism with his New Economic Policy called 'state capitalism'. The state owned key industries, public utilities and financial institutions under this system. Small-scale industry and farming remained in private hands.

The Russian Soviet Federal Socialist Republic (RSFSR) joined Ukraine, Belorussia, Georgia, Armenia and Azerbaijan in 1922 to form the Union of Soviet Socialist Republics, the USSR or Soviet Union. A constitution for the union was adopted in 1924.

When Lenin died in 1924 , the leadership of the party and the government was split between Leon Trotsky and Joseph Stalin. Trotsky wanted to spread communism worldwide. The more practical Stalin wanted to consolidate the domestic position. Stalin emerged victorious and Trotsky was exiled in 1928.

Stalin ended the New Economic Policy in 1928. He began the first of the five-year plans, calling for swift acceleration of industrial development and the collectivization of farms. The more prosperous peasants, called kulaks, withheld grain in protest, but they were liquidated and their lands seized. The collectivization of farms was chaotic, causing widespread famine in 1932–33.

The 1934 party congress began moves to depose Stalin and replace him with Sergei Kirov. Kirov was assassinated the following December. Stalin launched a wide-ranging purge of anyone who opposed him from 1935 to 1939. Senior party officials were tortured into false confessions. Millions of other members were executed or sent to labor camps.

The Soviet Union made concerted attempts to improve relationships with other countries. It was admitted to the League of Nations in 1934. Russia signed a non-aggression pact with Nazi Germany on August 23, 1939. It included a secret agreement for dividing various parts of eastern Europe between the Soviet Union and Germany.

Germany then invaded Poland, leading Britain and France to declare war against it in September 1939. Soviet forces also invaded Poland, which was then partitioned. Lithuania, Estonia and Latvia on the Baltic coast were all occupied by Soviet forces. Attempts to do the same with Finland resulted in a war lasting into 1941. Soviet forces finally prevailed against the fierce Finnish defense.

Germany surprised the Soviet Union by ignoring the non-aggression pact and invading the USSR on June 22, 1941. Supported by Romania, Hungary, Slovakia, Italy and Finland, the German forces came close to capturing Moscow. The United States and Britain extended aid to the USSR. the United States alone supplied

FLAT EARTH PICTURE GALLERY

The ornate GUM department store in Moscow.

some $12 billion worth of equipment.

The war turned into a long and bitter fight as Soviet forces resisted. Millions of Soviet citizens were killed. Nonetheless, Moscow and Stalingrad (the renamed St. Petersburg) held out against German sieges. Over 300,000 German troops surrendered at Stalingrad in February of 1943.

The Red Army then pushed the Germans west, capturing large areas of the Balkans and Poland. Soviet forces entered the outskirts of Berlin in April 1945. U.S. and Soviet troops met at the Elba River shortly thereafter. The war had ended.

The Soviet Union came to dominate many eastern European nations after the war. Czechoslovakia, Poland and Hungary all adopted communist-style governments.

World War II gave way to the Cold War between the Soviet Union and the Western Allies. Each side struggled to influence the political direction of smaller countries. The world became split into three camps. The First World comprised the United States and its allies, the Second World was the Soviet Union and its supporters and the Third World was all nations not aligned with either.

Stalin died in 1953. He was replaced by a collective leadership. The power of the secret police was curtailed. Georgei Malenkov was premier until 1953, when he was replaced by Nikolai Bulganin. Nikita Khruschchev, first secretary of the Communist Party of the Soviet Union, became premier in 1958. Kruschchev decentralized control of agriculture and modernized some of the bureaucracy.

Khrushchev began a major effort to discredit Joseph Stalin. He spoke out against the former leader's treatment of high-ranking members of the Communist party. He had Stalin's portraits removed from public places. Institutions and places bearing his name were renamed. Textbooks were rewritten to deflate Stalin's reputation.

International tension increased when the Soviet Union exploded its first nuclear weapon. The Soviet space program sent a satellite, Sputnik, into orbit in 1957. The Soviets were also first with a manned space flight when Yuri Gagarin orbited the earth in 1961.

Relations with China deteriorated in the late 1950s. China accused the Soviet Union of weakening its advocacy for communism.

Khruschchev moved to establish missile bases in Cuba in 1962. This provoked a major

Russia

High-rise accomodation typical of the Soviet era.

confrontation in October between the Soviet leader and President John Kennedy of the United States. Kruschchev finally abandoned his plan when he realized the extent of Kennedy's determination. Ships carrying the missiles were ordered to turn back from Cuba.

Dissatisfaction with Krushchev's style was growing within the Communist Party. He was replaced by Leonid Brezhnev as party secretary and Aleksey Kosygin as premier in October 1964. Brezhnev re-centralized many functions of the government. Intellectuals who protested against government policies were exiled.

The split with China deepened during the Vietnam War. The Soviet Union supplied huge amounts of material and financial aid to the North Vietnamese. China's relations with North Vietnam were very cool. Soviet troops invaded Czechoslovakia in 1968 to suppress growing liberalization, sparking worldwide condemnation.

United States president Richard Nixon visited Moscow in 1972. This began the period of détente with the west. Discussions led to an agreement on the partial limitation of strategic nuclear weapons, and agreements to cooperate on trade and space exploration.

FLAT EARTH PICTURE GALLERY

This ultimately led to the signing of the SALT treaty in 1979.

Following the assassination of President Muhammad Daoud Khan of Afghanistan in 1979, Brezhnev ordered his troops to invade that country. Despite its superior weaponry and manpower, the huge Soviet force was no match for United States-supported guerrilla bands. Much of the rest of the world opposed the Soviet action, which continued for ten years. Many countries and individual athletes boycotted the 1980 Moscow Olympic Games.

Brezhnev died in November of 1982. Yuri Andropov became general secretary and head of state. He died in early 1984. His successor, Konstantin Chernenko, died in March 1985. Mikhail Gorbachev became general secretary. At fifty-four, he was the youngest member of the Politburo.

Gorbachev's liberal policies of glasnost (openness) and perestroika (restructuring) shook the Soviet Union to its foundations. Large numbers of aged bureaucrats were removed from government positions.

International relations improved and the threat of nuclear war began to diminish. Summit meetings with U. S. President Ronald Reagan led both countries to eliminate a large portion of their nuclear arsenals. Soviet forces were withdrawn from Afghanistan in February 1989.

Constitutional amendments introduced free elections for the new Congress of People's Deputies in 1988. Reformers swept the polls, deposing the old Communist Party faithfuls. The Congress elected Gorbachev chairman of the Supreme Soviet on May 25, 1989. Spirits were high, but there were growing problems with the economy. Its structure was stalled in outdated policies. Gorbachev did not work to overturn the government-controlled economy in favor of a market economy. The nation was caught somewhere in the middle. Food shortages, high prices and strikes were commonplace.

Following a referendum in March of 1991, the office of president was introduced to Russia. Boris Yeltsin was elected president.

Other communist nations broke with the Soviet Union. Most made the change to a market economy far more efficiently. The Baltic states demanded independence.

Communist reactionaries led by Vice-President Gennady Yanayev, detained Gorbachev in the Crimea in August of 1991. Gorbachev was about to sign an agreement giving autonomy to the Soviet republics. The coup was poorly planned and coordinated. President Boris Yeltsin led opposition to the plot, which collapsed on August 21st. Gorbachev signed the new agreement after being freed. It all but eliminated the office of Soviet president, passing real power to the presidents of the constituent republics.

President Yeltsin banned the Communist Party on August 23rd. The Congress of People's Deputies dissolved the Soviet Union in September of 1991. A transitional government was

A rural windmill, reminiscent of an earlier time in Russian history.

Russia

established, in which a State Council exercised emergency powers. The following day the council recognized Lithuania, Latvia and Estonia as independent nations. Former republics established the Commonwealth of Independent States (CIS). Gorbachev resigned on December 25, and the Soviet acknowledged the dissolution of the USSR on December 26.

Yeltsin was seen as responsible for the end of the Soviet Union. As Russian president, he was leader of the most powerful republic. Yeltsin continued Gorbachev's work, but with more urgency. Hampered by former communists in the parliament, he called for new elections in September 1993. The parliament reacted by naming Aleksandr Rutskoi acting president in Yeltsin's place.

Anti-Yeltsin groups barricaded themselves inside the parliament building. Their supporters attacked strategic sites around Moscow. The military launched an attack in October, taking the parliament building after a fierce battle. A new constitution, adopted in December, gave greater power to the president.

The region of Chechnya became a trouble spot for Russia in 1994. Separatist guerrillas were demanding greater autonomy. The Russian military's action, widely condemned as excessively brutal, failed to stop the separatists' demands. Tens of thousands of civilians were killed. Thousands more were displaced. A peace accord was signed in 1997.

The government of Russia faced several difficulties during 1999. It became involved in a dispute with NATO over actions to cease the persecution of ethnic Albanians in Kosovo. President Yeltsin made major changes in his cabinet four times during a seventeen-month period. A Muslim separatist movement in Dagestan required a major military assault.

Yeltsin resigned as president in December of 1999 and Vladimir Putin became acting president. Putin went on to win the March 2000 presidential election decisively.

Putin has substantial economic and social challenges facing him. Many Russian people yearn for a return to the policies of the Soviet Union. The market economy has been a bonanza for some and a disaster for others. Domination of many aspects of Russian business by criminal organizations is also a major issue. Problems associated with the disposal of old nuclear weapons and obsolete nuclear-powered submarines continue.

FLAT EARTH PICTURE GALLERY

Spassky Tower, part of the Kremlin complex in Moscow.

Rwanda

REPUBLIC OF RWANDA

GOVERNMENT
Website
www.rwanda1.com/government
Capital Kigali
Type of government Republic
Independence from Belgium
(UN Trust Territory)
July 1, 1962
Voting Universal adult suffrage
Head of state President
Head of government Prime
Minister
Constitution 1995
Legislature Unicameral
Transitional National Assembly
Judiciary Supreme Court
Member of IMF, OAU, UN,
UNESCO, WHO, WTO

LAND AND PEOPLE
Land area 10,169 sq mi
(26,338 sq km)
Highest point
Volcan Karisimbi
14,780 ft (4,505 m)
Population 7,312,756
Major cities and populations
Kigal 369,000
Ethnic groups
Hutu 80%, Tutsi 19%, Twa 1%
Religions
Christianity 65%, traditional
animism25%
Languages
Kinyarwanda, French, English (all
official), indigenous languages

ECONOMIC
Currency Rwandan franc
Industry
cement, beverages, soap, furniture,
footwear, plastic goods, textiles
Agriculture
coffee, tea, pyrethrum, bananas,
beans, sorghum, potatoes, livestock
Natural resources
gold, tin, wolframite, methane

Rwanda is a tiny landlocked country in east-central Africa. The center of the country is a high, hilly plateau. A mountain system faces the west side of the plateau, with volcanoes on the northernmost end. The land slopes down to a series of marshy lakes along the upper Kagera River on the east. The tropical climate is modified by the high altitudes. Rainfall is heaviest in the west.

Eighty percent of Rwandans are Hutu, the balance being Tutsi. The Pygmy Twa form a tiny minority. Two-thirds of the people are Christian. Many others follow traditional indigenous beliefs. French, English and Kinyarwanda are the official languages.

Hutu farmers migrated to Rwanda in the 1300s, displacing the Twa Pygmies. Tutsi arrived from the south during the fifteenth century. They established control over the Twa and Hutu.

John Hanning Spack was the first European to visit the area in 1858. German explorers and missionaries followed. Rwanda and nearby Urundi (now Burundi) became part of German East Africa around 1890. Indigenous leaders maintained generally good relations with the Germans. Belgian forces took control in 1916.

The League of Nations mandated the territory to Belgium after World War I. Belgians named the region Ruanda-Urundi.

Hutu revolutionaries deposed the Tutsi monarchy in 1959 and won the 1960 election. Belgium granted independence on July 1, 1960, with Grégoire Kayibanda as president. Kayibanda was deposed by Major-General Juvénal Habyarimana in 1973

Multiple political parties were permitted from 1991. A power-sharing agreement between the Tutsi and the Hutu provoked violence.

Habyarimana died in a suspicious aircraft crash in 1994. Rwandan soldiers and Hutu gangs went on a killing spree. Close to one million people, mostly Tutsis, died. A United Nations peacekeeping force was sent in. The Tutsi Rwandan Political Front (RPF) seized control of Rwanda, appointing Pasteur Bizimungu as president. Two million Hutus fled the country.

More than 100,000 Hutu refugees died of disease and malnutrition in Zairean refugee camps. The United Nations has been indicting participants in the 1994 genocide, but progress has been slow.

Returning Hutu refugees clashed with the army and rebel groups. A power struggle forced Bizimungu to resign in 2000. His replacement was Paul Kagame, a Tutsi. A major International Monetary Fund/World Bank debt relief program began in 2001.

Saint Kitts and Nevis

FEDERATION OF SAINT KITTS AND NEVIS

A federation of two islands, Saint Kitts and Nevis is located in the eastern Caribbean. It is at the northern end of the Leeward Islands. Both islands, formed by volcanic activity, have considerable fertile farmland and a reliable water supply. The islands lie in the Caribbean hurricane zone. Temperatures, moderated by sea breezes, remain fairly consistent throughout the year.

Almost all the population is descended from slaves brought from Africa in colonial times. Christianity is the dominant religion. English, the official language, is often spoken in a modified form.

Agriculture is the principal economic activity. Sugar and molasses are the chief products. Fruits, coconuts and vegetables are also grown. Tourism is steadily growing as foreign investors build new and elaborate facilities. Saint Kitts and Nevis has one of the largest electronics assembly industries in the Caribbean.

Financial services have grown due to liberal banking laws. International charges of money laundering have prompted the government to install more efficient methods of monitoring financial transactions.

Arawak and Carib peoples settled both islands well before the arrival of Europeans. Christopher Columbus landed on the islands in 1493. They were settled by the British in 1623 and 1628, respectively. Sugar and cotton planting commenced and slaves were brought from Africa. Saint Kitts was seized by the French several times in the seventeenth and eighteenth centuries. It was ceded to Great Britain by the Treaty of Paris in 1783.

Anguilla, Saint Kitts and Nevis were united as a British dependency in 1871. Voting for all adults was granted in 1951. The Leeward Islands was included in the ill-fated Federation of the West Indies from 1958 to 1962. Internal self-government was granted in 1967, with Robert Bradshaw as premier.

Anguilla was placed under direct British rule in 1971. It officially withdrew from the dependency in 1980.

Saint Kitts and Nevis became independent on September 19, 1983, as a member of the Commonwealth of Nations. The British monarch is its head of state.

Separatist movements on Nevis have grown in recent years. A referendum in 1998 that would have made Nevis an independent state fell only very slightly short of the necessary two-thirds majority.

Hurricane Georges struck the islands in 1998, causing more than $400 million in property damage. Thousands of people lost their homes.

They were also identified in 2001 as havens for money laundering.

GOVERNMENT
Website www.stkittsnevis.net
Capital Basseterre
Type of government
Constitutional monarchy
Independence from Britain
September 19, 1983
Voting Universal adult suffrage
Head of state
British Crown,
represented by Governor-General
Head of government Prime Minister
Constitution 1983
Legislature
Unicameral National Assembly
Judiciary
Eastern Caribbean Supreme Court
Member of Caricom, CN, IMF, OAS, UN, UNESCO, WHO, WTO

LAND AND PEOPLE
Land area 101 sq mi (261 sq km)
Highest point Mt. Misery
4,314 ft (1,315 m)
Coastline 84 mi (135 km)
Population 38,756
Major cities and populations
Basseterre 12,600
Ethnic groups African 96%, Mulatto 3%, European 1%
Religion Christianity
Languages
English (official), English Creole

ECONOMIC
Currency East Caribbean dollar
Industry
sugar milling, tourism, cotton, salt, copra, clothing, footwear, beverages
Agriculture
sugar cane, rice, yams, vegetables, bananas
Natural resources

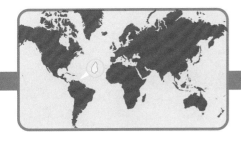

Saint Lucia

Saint Lucia is an island in the eastern Caribbean Sea, the second largest of the Windward Islands group. It was originally formed by volcanic activity. A chain of heavily forested mountains runs north to south. The mountains are separated by several fertile river valleys. A volcanic crater near the town of Soufriere has hot sulfur springs, which supply geothermal energy. The climate is tropical with high temperatures and humidity year round. A rainy season occurs from May to August.

Almost all of the population is of African descent. There is a small minority of people whose ancestor came from India. Most of the people are Catholic. English is the official language. Many Saint Lucians speak a French patois.

The economy of Saint Lucia is largely dependent upon agriculture. Bananas are the most important crop, followed by coconuts and mangoes. The manufacturing sector produces electronic goods, apparel and beverages. Tourism is important and has been steadily growing since the 1960s.

Saint Lucia was first settled by Arawak people and later by Caribs. Both groups migrated from South America. British and French settlers arrived on the island during the 1600s. The French were more successful, reaching an agreement with the Caribs in 1660. Britain regularly contested French ownership. The question was finally settled in Britain's favor in the wake of the Napoleonic Wars in Europe, in 1814.

Banana growing quickly became the main economic activity. Slaves were brought from Africa to work on the plantations.

Representative government was introduced in 1924. Saint Lucia was administered as part of the British Windward Islands until 1958. It was included with most other British Caribbean colonies in the West Indies Federation from 1958 to 1962.

Saint Lucia was grouped with five other colonies as the West Indies Associated States in 1967. It gained independence in its own right on February 22, 1979, as a member of the Commonwealth of Nations. The United Workers Party was defeated in 1997, after holding office for all but three years since 1964. The Labour Party has prevailed since that time.

A crisis over the export of bananas to Europe badly damaged the economy in the late 1990s. The dispute has since been resolved. International regulatory agencies accused Saint Lucia and many other Caribbean island nations of participation in money laundering and other fraudulent financial activities in 2001.

St. Vincent & the Grenadines

Saint Vincent and the Grenadines is a group of islands in the Windward Islands in the Caribbean Sea. Saint Vincent is the large island, while the Grenadines is a group of much smaller islands to the south. Saint Vincent is mountainous, with lush cover of rainforests. The volcano La Soufrière erupted in 1812, 1902 and 1979, causing substantial damage and loss of life. The temperature averages 76°F. (24°C.) throughout the year. Coastals areas get a good deal of rain. Interior regions get more than twice as much.

The majority of the population is descended from African slaves brought to the islands during colonial times. Many others have a mixture of African and European heritages. Most of the people are Christian, with the Anglican Church the most prevalent denomination. English is the official language, but a French patois is widely spoken.

Arawaks were the first inhabitants of the islands. They were later displaced by Caribs arriving from South America. Although the European colonial powers knew of the islands, none made an effort to claim them. British planters had established themselves on Saint Vincent and imported African slaves as laborers by 1762.

France captured the Saint Vincent in 1779, but returned it to the British settlers four years later. The Carib people revolted against British control in 1796. Britain deported most of them to its Honduras colony. Following Britain's abolition of slavery in the 1830s, indentured laborers were imported from India.

Saint Vincent became part of the British Windward Islands in 1880. It was a member of the Federation of the West Indies from 1958 to 1962.

Internal self-government was introduced in 1969. Full independence was granted to Saint Vincent and the Grenadines on October 27, 1979. Milton Cato was the first prime minister and the British monarch was head of state.

The government clashed with the British Foreign Office in the late 1990s over allegations that the country was being used for money laundering by illegal drug traffickers. International regulatory agencies also labelled the country, along with many other Caribbean nations, as a suspected haven for tax evasion and narcotics trade.

High unemployment and a U.S.-Europe trade dispute over bananas plagued the nation's economy in the late 1990s. Elections in 2001 ended 17 years of New Democratic party government. Ralph Gonsalves of the Unity Party became prime minister.

GOVERNMENT
Capital Kingstown
Type of government
Constitutional monarchy
Independence from Britain
October 27, 1979
Voting Universal adult suffrage
Head of state
British Crown,
represented by Governor-General
Head of government Prime Minister
Constitution 1979
Legislature
Unicameral House of Assembly
Judiciary
Eastern Caribbean Supreme Court
Member of Caricom, CN, IMF, OAS, UN, UNESCO, UNHCR, WTO

LAND AND PEOPLE
Land area 150 sq mi (389 sq km)
Highest point Soufriere
4,048 ft (1,234 m)
Coastline 52 mi (84 km)
Population 116,394
Major cities and populations
Kingstown 28,000
Ethnic groups
African 82%, others 18%
Religions Christianity
Languages
English (official), French patois

ECONOMIC
Currency East Caribbean dollar
Industry
food processing, cement, furniture, clothing
Agriculture
bananas, coconuts, sweet potatoes, spices, livestock
Natural resources

Samoa

INDEPENDENT STATE OF SAMOA

Samoa is in the southern Pacific Ocean northeast of New Zealand. Savai'i and Upolu, the coral-fringed main islands, are volcanic in origin, with mountainous inland areas. Fast-flowing rivers descend through thick rainforests to narrow coastal plains. The climate is tropical, with high temperatures and humidity all year.

Most of the population is of Polynesian descent. About ten percent are of mixed European–Polynesian heritage. Samoa is strongly Christian. English and Samoan are the official languages.

Samoa was settled as early as 1000 B.C. by Polynesian people. Fijian tribes invaded in the thirteenth century A.D. Jacob Roggeveen arrived from the Netherlands in 1722. French explorer Louis Antoine de Bougainville named the group the Navigator Islands in 1768.

European adventurers and fortune-seekers disrupted traditional village life in the following decades. Christianity was brought to Samoa by the London Missionary Society in 1830.

Britain, Germany and the United States established commercial posts in Samoa during the nineteenth century. The United States established a naval coaling station at Pago Pago in 1878.

Famed author Robert Louis Stevenson settled on Samoa in 1889. He was suffering from tuberculosis. Five years later, he died and was buried there. Samoans called him tusitala, or teller of stories.

The selection of a king caused major confrontations among native peoples in the late 1800s. The three countries with interests on the islands didn't know which one should intervene or in what manner. The Act of Berlin, in 1889, gave the islands independence. A native civil war followed.

The United States, Germany and Britain reached an agreement regarding control of the islands. The western islands were annexed to Germany in 1899. The islands were occupied by New Zealand during World War I.

New Zealand troops removed Western Samoa from German control in 1914. It was granted a mandate over the territory by the League of Nations in 1920. Nationalist groups began agitating for independence during the following years. The constitution was written to combine traditional Samoan tribal structures and British-style democracy. The islands became independent on January 1, 1962.

A treaty secured New Zealand's aid in international matters. The national assembly passed a constitutional amendment changing the country's name from Western Samoa to Samoa on July 4, 1997.

San Marino

MOST SERENE REPUBLIC OF SAN MARINO

This small enclave is located within central Italy, east of the city of Florence. The main geographical feature is Mount Titano, one of the Apennines Mountains, which rises to an elevation of 2,457 feet (749 kilometers). The Ausa, Marano and San Marino rivers run through the republic. The climate is temperate. Winters are cool and summers are warm.

Close to ninety percent of the people are Sanmarinesi. The rest are Italian. Around 10,000 Sanmarinesi live outside the republic. Almost the entire population is Christian, and virtually all are Catholic. Italian is the official language. There is a distinct Sanmarinese dialect.

The economy of San Marino is based on tourism and agriculture. Wheat, wine, livestock and dairy products dominate the agricultural output. Building stone is quarried. Manufactures include textiles, clothing, electronic goods and ceramics. The crafting of gold and silver jewelry and the sale of postage stamps are also significant.

San Marino's legislature is the Great and General Council. Its 60 members are elected by the people for five years. Two members of the council, called captains-regent, are elected to preside over an executive body called the Congress of State.

A Christian stonemason named Marinus sought refuge from religious persecution on Mt. Titano in the fourth century A.D. He established a community there. It is claimed to be the world's first republic. It gradually evolved into a tiny state, despite attempts by various rulers from neighboring Rimini who wanted to gain control. Pope Nicholas V recognized San Marino's independence in 1291.

Following the Risorgimento period in the nineteenth century, Italy was unified into a single state. San Marino declined to join it. A friendship and cooperation treaty was negotiated with Italy in 1862.

Fascists gained control in 1923. They followed Italy's lead by declaring war on Britain in 1940. When Italy surrendered to the Allies three years later, the fascists were deposed. Although San Marino had declared itself neutral, German forces invaded during 1944.

San Marino was ruled by a coalition of Communists and Socialists from 1945 to 1957. The Christian Democratic Party, aided by Communist dissidents, took control in 1957. Communists again came to power in 1978. A new Christian Democrat-Communist coalition was formed in 1986.

The republic has retained its independent status. San Marino joined the United Nations in 1992. It remains the world's smallest republic.

GOVERNMENT
Type of government Republic
Voting Universal adult suffrage
Head of state and government
Captains-Regent, leading the Congress of State
Legislature
Unicameral Grand and General Council
Judiciary Council of Twelve
Member of
CE, IMF, UN, UNESCO, WHO, WTO

LAND AND PEOPLE
Land area 24 sq mi (61 sq km)
Highest point Monte Titano 2,457 ft (749 m)
Population 27,336
Ethnic groups
Sanmarinesi 88%, Italian 12%
Religion Christianity
Languages Italian (official)

ECONOMIC
Currency Euro
Industry
tourism, banking, textiles, electronics, ceramics, cement, wine, philately
Agriculture
wheat, grapes, corn, olives, cattle, pigs, horses, beef, dairy
Natural resources
construction stone

São Tomé and Príncipe

DEMOCRATIC REPUBLIC OF SÃO TOMÉ AND PRÍNCIPE

GOVERNMENT
Capital São Tomé
Type of government Republic
Independence from Portugal
July 12, 1975
Voting Universal adult suffrage
Head of state President
Head of government Prime
Minister
Constitution 1990
Legislature
Unicameral National Assembly
Judiciary Supreme Court
Member of
IMF, OAU, UN, UNESCO, WHO

LAND AND PEOPLE
Land area 400 sq mi
(960 sq km)
Highest point
Pico de São Tomé
6,640 ft (2,024 m)
Coastline 130 mi (209 km)
Population 165,034
Major cities and populations
São Tomé 43,000
Trinidade 12,000
Ethnic groups
Descendants of freed slaves
Religions Christianity
Languages Portuguese (official),
indigenous languages

ECONOMIC
Currency Dobra
Industry
textiles, soap, beverages,
seafood processing, timber
Agriculture
cacao, coconuts, palm kernels,
copra, cinnamon, pepper, coffee,
bananas, papayas, beans, poultry
Natural resources
seafood

Two larger islands and four rocky islets make up São Tomé and Príncipe in the Gulf of Guinea, off the western African coast. The volcanic landscape is heavily forested. There are coastal lowlands in the north and south of each island. The climate is tropical, with high temperatures and humidity. There is a rainy season from October to May.

Most of the people are descended from slaves brought from the African mainland hundreds of years ago. The small European population includes Portuguese and numerous foreign contract laborers. Most of people are Christians, predominantly Catholics. Portugese is the official language. Various indigenous languages are spoken.

Portuguese explorers arrived in the 1470s. A settlement was established on São Tomé in 1485 as a supply base for ships sailing to Asia. It became a Portuguese colony during the sixteenth century.

Sugar cane plantations were established. Slaves were brought from the African mainland. Cacao became the dominant crop by the nineteenth century. European countries, which had begun banning slavery, wanted to discourage it worldwide. The terrible conditions labor conditions on plan- were exposed in Europe during 1905. A trading ban on São Tomé and Príncipe cacao followed. Conditions improved, but planters continued treating workers as slaves.

Many African nations started agitating for independence during the 1950s. A groups of São Toméans formed the Movement for the Liberation of São Tomé and Príncipe (MLSTP) Its membership grew through the 1960s. When Portugal's government fell to an army coup in 1974, the MLSTP sought independence. Independence was won on July 7, 1975 Manuel Pinto da Costa was chosen as president.

Depressed prices for cacao created economic problems in the 1980s. A coup attempt by mercenaries from Gabon was defeated in 1978. Another coup ten years later was similarly suppressed. The new constitution of 1991 ended one-party elections. Independent Miguel Trovoada defeated the MLSTP's candidate to become president.

A coup staged in August 1995 by army officers removed Trovoada from office. He was restored shortly afterwards, following Angolan intervention. The World Bank agreed to a U.S. $200 million debt reduction program to aid São Tomé and Príncipe's ailing economy in 2000. The new Independent Democratic Action party prevailed in the 2001 elections.

Saudi Arabia

KINGDOM OF SAUDI ARABIA

Saudi Arabia is on the far western edge of Asia. It has two long coastlines, one on the Red Sea in the west, another on the Persian Gulf in the east. It occupies eighty percent of the Arabian Peninsula. The narrow coastal plains along the Red Sea rise to a mountain range which runs northwest to southeast. The Great Sandy Desert lies across much of the south. Most of Saudi Arabia is arid or semi-arid desert. The climate is hot and dry with minimal rainfall.

Ninety percent of the people are Arabs. The remainder are of mixed African–Asian heritage. Virtually all of the people are Wahhabi Muslims. Saudi Arabia is home to Mecca, birthplace of the prophet Muhammad. As many as two million Muslims from all over the world make the pilgrimage to Mecca and Medina each year. Arabic is the official language.

Saudi Arabia's economy is based primarily on oil. Saudi Arabia is the world's leading oil exporter. The industry is concentrated in the northeast near the Persian Gulf. Petroleum revenues account for 90 percent of all export income.

The power of Saudi Arabia's king is absolute. There is no parliament and no written constitution. The legal and social systems are based on the Koran and Sharia law. The king is advised by an appointed council of ministers. The line of royal succession is ill-defined. Usually a prince is selected and approved by the royal family and religious leaders.

The Arabian Peninsula was home to nomadic tribes before 3000 B.C. The Minaen kingdom was well established near the Red Sea by 500 B.C.

The prophet Muhammad was born in Mecca in 570 A.D. He founded Islam in the seventh century. Most of the

The Al-Aan Palace at Najran, a typical Saudi mudbrick structure.

LONELY PLANET IMAGES — TONY WHEELER

peninsula's population embraced the new faith within a short time. Arabia declined as the center of Islam after Muhammad's death in 632. A disagreement over succession led to a split among Muslims. The Shi'ites believed that heredity should determine succession. Sunnis believed the leader should be elected. Muhammad's followers went on to conquer and convert the entire Middle East. The caliphate was established first at Damascus, then in Baghdad.

The Mamelukes from Egypt took control in 1269. The Ottoman Turks gained control of it when they conquered Egypt in 1517. They were unable to extend their authority to the interior of the land.

A Muslim preacher named Muhammad Ibn Abd al-Wahhab came to prominence in 1744. His followers established an Arab state in the Najd region. The Wahhabis captured Mecca in 1812. Riyadh became their capital in 1818. The 21-year-old Abdul Azizibn Saud began his conquest and unification of Arabia. He captured region after region from 1913 to 1926. Saud announced the creation of the Kingdom of Saudi Arabia in 1932. He was its king. The new nation would be ruled under strict Islamic principles.

The Arabian American Oil Company (Aramco) struck oil in the Saudi desert in 1936. It was soon apparent that Saudi Arabia held vast oil reserves. Production began in 1938. Royalties from oil increased rapidly. King Ibn Saud developed extensive modernization programs in areas such as water supply, agriculture, manufacturing, and public health.

Saudi Arabia supported the Allied cause during World War II. It permitted the construction of a U.S. air base near Dhahran. It remained neutral until March of 1945, when it declared war on Germany and Japan. Saudi Arabia joined the Arab League in 1945, the same year it became a founding member of the United Nations.

King Ibn Saud died in 1953. He was succeeded by his son, Saud. A Council of Ministers was created to advise the king, who appointed all its members. The new King Ibn Saud signed a mutual-defense pact with Egypt in 1955. He granted a $10 million loan to Syria for economic and military purposes. He also made a loan of $10 million to Egypt during the 1956 Suez crisis.

Relations with Egypt began to deteriorate in 1962. Egypt supported a revolution against the government of Yemen. Saud had extended aid to the overthrown Yemeni imam. Saudi Arabia attacked Yemen, then Egypt bombed Saudi Arabian towns. Saudi Arabia severed diplomatic ties with Egypt.

GOVERNMENT
Website www.saudinf.com
Capital Riyadh
Type of government Absolute monarchy
Voting none
Head of state Monarch
Head of government Monarch
Constitution 1993
Legislature Appointed Consultative Council
Judiciary Supreme Council of Justice
Member of AL, IMF, OPEC, UN, UNESCO, WHO

LAND AND PEOPLE
Land area 865,000 sq mi (2,240,000 sq km)
Highest point Jabal Sawda 10,279 ft (3,133 m)
Coastline 1,640 mi (2,640 km)
Population 22,757,092
Major cities and populations
Riyadh 3,300,000
Jiddah 1,800,000
Mecca 910,000
Ethnic groups
Arab 90%, African-Asian 10%
Religion Islam
Languages Arabic (official)

ECONOMIC
Currency Riyal
Industry
oil production, petroleum refining, petrochemicals, cement, fertilizer, plastics
Agriculture
wheat, barley, sugar cane, fruits, beef cattle, sheep, wool, poultry, dairy
Natural resources
petroleum, natural gas, iron ore, gold, copper

Saudi Arabia

Saud's extravagance had plunged his country into economic turmoil.

King Saud was forced to step down in 1964. His brother Faisal became king. Faisal exploited Saudi Arabia's vast wealth, adopting appropriate technology and expertise from the west without compromising basic Islamic values.

Saudi Arabia was not a military participant in the Arab–Israeli wars of 1967 and 1973. It did lead the subsequent oil embargo. It was able to control overall policy within the Organization of Petroleum Exporting Countries (OPEC). Oil prices soared under the embargo. This caused a crisis in the West, but it increased Saudia Arabia's wealth.

Faisal was assassinated by his nephew in 1975. His brother Khalid took the throne. Effective power lay with another brother named Fahd.

Saudi Arabia's guardianship of Islamic culture was challenged in November of 1979. Militant Wahhabis occupied the Great Mosque at Mecca. Sixty-three rebels were executed during and after weeks of fighting with Saudi military forces.

Shi'ite Muslims in Qatif became inspired by the 1979 Iranian revolution. Rioters demanding reforms were brutally suppressed. Some changes were made. Saudi Arabia supported Iraq in the 1980–88 war with Iran, in hope that the spirit of Iran's revolution would not further affect its own people.

Khalid died in 1982. He was replaced by Fahd. The Saudis deliberately cultivated good relations with the West, particularly the United States. Criticism of Saudi Arabia's repressive human rights record was muted by most of the Western nations. Economic ties were strengthened. Most wanted to remain friendly with such a large oil supplier.

Support for Iraq ended with the Iraqi invasion of Kuwait in 1990. King Fahd allowed coalition forces to use bases in Saudi Arabia. Large numbers of Saudi troops took part in the Gulf War in 1991. Terrorist bombings in Dhahran and Riyadh in 1995–96 killed a number of United States service personnel.

There was a broadening of responsibility for administering the country during the 1990s. This did not reduce the king's absolute power. Crown Prince Abdullah began ruling on behalf of the ailing Fahd by the early 2000s.

The September 2001 attacks on the United States put a strain on relations with Saudi Arabia. Fifteen of the nineteen terrorists involved in those attacks were Saudi citizens. The leader of the plot, Osama bin Laden, was from a prominent Saudi family. The U.S. did not blame Saudi Arabia for the attacks, but did voice concern about its financial support of leftist Islamic groups and its apparent hesitation to take part in the United States' war against terrorism. Saudi Arabia did gain international support for its 2002 efforts to develop diplomatic ties with Israel.

Traditional Saudi housing at Jeddah.

Sénégal

REPUBLIC OF SENEGAL

GOVERNMENT
Website www.gouv.sn
Capital Dakar
Type of government Republic
Independence from France
June 20, 1960
Voting Universal adult suffrage
Head of state President
Head of government Prime
Minister
Constitution 1901
Legislature
Unicameral National Assembly
Judiciary Constitutional Court
Member of IMF, OAU, UN,
UNESCO, WHO, WTO

LAND AND PEOPLE
Land area 75,750 sq mi
(196,192 sq km)
Highest point
unnamed location 1,907 ft (581 m)
Coastline 330 mi (531 km)
Population 10,284,929
Major cities and populations
Dakar 2,080,000
Thiès 225,000
Kaolack 200,000
Ethnic groups Wolof 48%, Fulani
14%, Serer 12%, Tukulor 8%,
Diola 5%, Mandingo 4%, others 9%
Religions Islam 94%, Christianity
5%, traditional animism 1%
Languages
French (official), indigenous
languages

ECONOMIC
Currency CFA franc
Industry
agricultural processing,
shipbuilding, seafood processing,
mining, fertilizer, petroleum
refining
Agriculture
peanuts, millet, corn, sorghum, rice,
cotton, tomatoes, vegetables,
livestock
Natural resources
seafood, phosphates, iron ore

Sénégal, on the western coast of Africa, is mostly low-lying grassland and semi-arid desert. The landscape rises progressively towards the border with Guinea. Temperatures are consistently high throughout the year.

The largest of Sénégal's ethnic groups is the Wolof, which makes up nearly half of the population. Other large groups are the Fulani, Serer, Tukulor and Diola. Ninety percent are Sunni Muslims. Most others are Christian. French is the official language. Each ethnic group has its own language.

Serer and Wolof peoples, Sénégal's original inhabitants, were part of the empire of ancient Ghana. They were joined by Tukulor people in the ninth century A.D. Islam was introduced in the eleventh century by the Berber Almovarid dynasty. The Mali Empire encompassed Sénégal for part of the fourteenth century.

Portuguese merchants established coastal trading posts in the fifteenth century. They were displaced by the French and Dutch shortly thereafter. The French prevailed for the next 100 years. Growth of the Fulani state of Futa Toro along the Sénégal River weakened French control.

Britain captured the French trading posts during the Seven Years' War, which ended in 1763. They were later returned to the French. France was successful in gaining power over the Wolof, Serer, and Tukulor regions during the nineteenth century.

Sénégal became a full colony in 1895 and formed the heart of French West Africa. Railways and ports were built to facilitate the booming peanut-growing trade.

Blaise Diagne, Sénégal's first African deputy, was elected to the French parliament in 1914. Sénégal became autonomous within the French Community in 1958. It achieved full independence as part of the Mali Federation, which joined Sénégal with the Sudanese Republic (now Mali) in June of 1960. Sénégal became a separate republic two months later.

A new constitution greatly enhanced President Léopold Senghor's powers after a 1962 coup attempt. Senghor's regime helped to diversify the economy. A multiparty system was adopted in 1976. Abdou Diouf became president in 1981.

Separatists in the Casamance region clashed with government forces from 1995 until a peace treaty was signed in March 2001. Sénégalese troops aided the government of Guinea-Bissau in the late 1990s. Abdoulaye Wade of the Sénégalese Democratic Party was elected president in 2000, ending forty years of Socialist Party rule.

Seychelles

REPUBLIC OF SEYCHELLES

The Seychelles is an archipelago of islands in the western Indian Ocean, northeast of the island of Madagascar. The country consists of two islands groups, the Mahé in the north and low-lying coral islands in the south. The forty islands of the Mahé group are formed of rock with hilly forested interiors rising to some 2,950 feet (900 meters). The country's principal islands belong to this group. More than 60 coral islands have no fresh water sources, and remain uninhabited. High temperatures and humidity prevail year round.

The Seychellois are a mixture of Asian, European and African heritages. Most of the people are Christian. English, French and Creole are the official languages.

Seychelles is one of Africa's most prosperous countries. Tourism, agriculture, and fishing are its principal industries. Leading exports include tuna, copra, and cinnamon bark. Tourism has grown increasingly since the international airport opened at Victoria in 1971. The country's offshore banking services are presently under investigation by international agencies.

The uninhabited Seychelles islands were discovered by Portuguese explorer Vasco Da Gama in 1502. France claimed the islands in 1756.

French planters and their slaves settled there beginning in 1768. Great Britain annexed the islands in 1794 and administered the islands from Mauritius during most of the 1800s.

The Seychelles became a crown colony in 1903. Plantation owners controlled the economy and the politics. Nationalist movements arose in the 1960s. The Democratic Party and the People's Independence Party were formed. Seychelles became independent on June 29, 1976. James Mancham became president with Albert René as prime minister.

One year later René deposed Mancham while he was out of the country. René declared the country a one-party state and a new constitution was adopted in 1979. René blamed Mancham for several later coup attempts. South African- based mercenaries tried to restore Mancham to office, but they were thwarted.

The army mutinied in 1982. Tanzanian troops restored order. Several more coup attempts were suppressed in the late 1980s.

Civil unrest led to constitutional amendments in the early 1990s. Multiparty elections were sanctioned. Albert René, leader of the People's Progressive Front since 1977, was reelected in 2001.

GOVERNMENT
Capital Victoria
Type of government Republic
Independence from Britain
June 28, 1976
Voting Universal adult suffrage
Head of state President
Head of government President
Constitution 1993
Legislature
Unicameral National Assembly
Judiciary Court of Appeal
Member of
CN, IMF, OAU, UN, UNESCO, WHO

LAND AND PEOPLE
Land area 176 sq mi (455 sq km)
Highest point
Morne Seychellois 2,969 ft (905 m)
Coastline 305 mi (491 km)
Population 79,715
Major cities and populations
Victoria 28,000
Ethnic groups
Seychellois 93%, Malagasy 3%,
Chinese 2%, European 2%
Religions Christianity 96%,
wothers 4%
Languages
Creole, French, English (all official)

ECONOMIC
Currency Seychelles rupee
Industry
fisheries, tourism, vanilla
processing, coir rope, boat building
Agriculture
coconuts, vanilla, sweet potatoes,
tapioca, bananas, poultry

Natural resources
seafood, copra, cinnamon